Kgb

The History Of The Eastern Most Infamous Intelligence Agencies

(The History And Legacy Of The Soviet Union Notorious Spy Agency)

Michael Peters

Published By **Riisas Honaka**

Michael Peters

Kgb: The History Of The Eastern Most Infamous Intelligence Agencies (The History And Legacy Of The Soviet Union Notorious Spy Agency)

ISBN   978-1-77485-643-7

Legal & Disclaimer

The information contained in this ebook is not designed to replace or take the place of any form of medicine or professional medical advice. The information in this ebook has been provided for educational & entertainment purposes only.

The information contained in this book has been compiled from sources deemed reliable, and it is accurate to the best of the Author's knowledge; however, the Author cannot guarantee its accuracy and validity and cannot be held liable for any errors or omissions. Changes are periodically made to this book. You must consult your doctor or get professional medical advice before using any of the

TABLE OF CONTENTS

Chapter 1: The Basic Principles Of Body

Language Secrets

Body language is a language that everyone uses everyday. It is a language that very few of us have conscious control over, but if we did and understood its powers we would gain so much more from our lives.

When I say body language I do not mean body movements that we consciously make like a wave, a handshake or perhaps a kiss, but all the micro movements that happen before and after our routine actions. These micro movements occur in a millisecond and are controllable by everyone with the knowledge to do so, but if we don't control them, we give away a massive amount of information about our mood, our intentions and very often the sincerity behind either an action or the spoken word.

Before we can begin to decrypt our own body language, we have to understand when the language is being used by others around us and when we are using it ourselves. Once armed with this information we are in the best position to quickly read others before they even speak or commit to an action and then adjust our own body language accordingly.

Using this simple decryption and then encryption philosophy, we can very quickly gain a real advantage in many situations, such as business, relationships and anywhere else you need or want to gain the pecuniary advantage.

A classic example of body language which I am sure we have all encountered is in the scenario of getting a Taxi. Perhaps from the airport or after a night out on the town.

Very often you will see a queue of Taxi drivers in the Taxi rank waiting for passengers. Along you come and there will be one that is really friendly looking and approachable and another who has his arms crossed does not make eye contact with you and overall he looks tired and uninterested.

Which one do you choose?

If you have been in this situation before I am sure you genuinely picked the friendly one. Keep in mind that you have already made your choice, without even speaking a single word.

If you have never experienced this then look out for it next time and you will see exactly what I mean.

Something that would have definitely happened at some stage to all of us would have occurred in a supermarket at the checkout desks. Have you noticed if you have the option of choosing which till to go to, which one it is that you finally choose?

I would like to bet that given the choice of two checkouts, one where the girl appears to be happy, alive and her face muscles are showing she is very much alert or one with a girl who is avoiding visual contact with you, her face muscles are relaxed, giving the appearance she is half asleep, you will choose the cheery girl?

Once again notice how we are making important decisions based upon what we see, not what we discuss or hear.

The first impressions with body language are the strongest impressions anyone can make. Huge decisions are made based upon what language your body is speaking and what language you interpret from others.

How many times have you gone for the perfect job, the job where absolutely everything stacks up in your favour, your skill set is exactly what the employer needs, the salary is right, your education is right, the interview went really well, then you received the call or letter to say they weren't interested. The reason you threw that opportunity away was not due to your Curriculum Vitae or what you said in the interview, it's what you didn't say that lost you the job, the non-verbal communication killed your chances!

These are all scenarios and situations we would have undoubtedly encountered and had we understood what was being silently said, we could have made our silent responses and gained the edge that we needed.

A scientific experiment was recently carried out in Germany. The experiment was conducted over two days with 10 people. On the first day all 10 people were served a three course meal, by a friendly waitress. Friendly as in smiling and giving out a bodily persona of friendliness, but she did not speak. All 10 people were served the same food per course.

On the second day a different waitress was used, this waitress had been kept up all night causing sleep deprivation and was instructed to serve the food in a tired and non-interested manner. All 10 people were served the same courses again, and the same food as the day previously.

The results were 9 people concluded that the food tasted better on the first day (despite all the food being exactly the same on both days) and 1 person voted for the food on the 2nd day. This one person had just come off of night shift and actually found synergy in being served by someone who was speaking the same lethargic body language as they were.

This is why when we are served in our own country or abroad by waiters and waitresses perhaps that do not speak are own language it is often the impression we take away from these places that we will not return to those establishments because the staff were rubbish. If we unravel the true reason behind this it is purely that because the staff don't or cannot speak English, we are relying solely upon their body language to determine how friendly and accommodating they are. If they have had a bad day or fail to use their body language correctly, we will not be returning to give that establishment our repeat custom.

Speech and language has been around for thousands of years, the most basic form of speech in the form of grunts, started in the Stone Age. Prior to this period and during the evolution of language as we know it today, the whole population relied completely on body language to communicate.

In the Stone Age people could tell instantly when someone approached them if they were friend or foe. In an instant just through body language they would determine if they were to greet the approaching person or to be ready to kill that person.

Of course we are no longer in the Stone Age, but our Presidents and Prime Ministers, have speeches specially prepared that show them exactly what body language to use and when, which in reflection is probably the best way to avoid out and out war by using the wrong body language at the wrong time as they might have done in the Stone Age.

It also shows us that these icons and leaders of our daily lives use body language to control us, to gain our vote or agreement of their policies and through this hidden language that we watch perhaps via a television they have complete control over us, until we know the secret.

We all have those exact same body language techniques built-in, we just need to nurture them, understand them and develop them once again.

It was the early part of 1967 while Alexander was completing his doctorate at university when he a received an unassuming telephone call that was to change his life.

Up until this call, Alexander had practiced his body language and psychology techniques in small workshop groups to help fund his way through university.

He told me that on the end of the phone was a male voice, with a distinct almost alarmed tone in his voice. The caller announced himself "Mr Ivankov, we have been following your workshops with great interest and wondered if you could help us with a government related issue". Alexander was not a glory hunter, but appreciated the recognition of his work and at this juncture in his life was just an ordinary guy trying to get through his university doctorate on a limited budget. Alexander hesitated before responding, which in itself is a great technique to procure more information. "Mr Ivankov, we have already cleared it with the university and if you choose to assist us we will pay you a fixed fee of 5,000 Rubles plus your expenses, plus a further 5,000 Rubles upon a successful conclusion". Well how could this struggling university student refuse, it was a huge amount of money and he would not have to give workshops for many years to come. "Yes, that sounds like a very attractive offer, what do I have to do?" The caller now with a much less alarmed tone in his voice said "we cannot discuss the case over a public telephone exchange; we will send a car to collect you at 0800 hrs. tomorrow morning. You will come to our offices to begin your studies. I look forward to meeting with you". Without chance for a reply the caller terminated the phone call.

Alexander was excited, yet nervous. Who was coming to collect him, where was he going, what did he have to do? So many questions, but no answers until the morning! He retired early to bed to ensure he was on top form knowing or in fact hoping that the offer of payment was genuine.

At 7.55am a car pulled up outside his apartment, peeking through the curtains he saw a solitary driver in the car, which appeared to be a Volga GAZ-24, there wasn't so many of these cars made at this time and those that were out of the production line were mainly owned by two types of people, the government and the KGB!

Alexander closed his apartment door and by the time he reached the car, the driver had left the drivers seat and was now opening the rear passenger door for him..such service.

Alexander greeted the driver and the driver wished him too a good morning before entering the vehicle and driving off. By now Alexander's questions were mounting up, but his primary one was where was he going to? He asked the driver and the polite response he received was that he could not be told, but would know when he arrived.

One hour later the car pulled up at Lubyanka Square in Moscow, Russia, directly outside a large Neo-Baroque building with a facade of yellow brick. This was the KGB headquarters. Now Alexander was a little nervous!

After going through security clearance and being presented with a visitors pass he was quickly ushered up to the 3rd floor and into a room with no windows and asked to sit. About 5 minutes later someone else entered the room and introduced himself as

Yuri Andropov. Mr Andropov produced a telex printout and placed it on the desk in front of him, "this is your bank account correct?". "Yes", more than a little concerned that the KGB knew his bank account details without volunteering the information. "Here is your latest statement and you will note the extra 5,000 Rubles balance as agreed". He looked at the statement in astonishment; his private bank account had been credited, overnight with 5,000 Rubles! If this was anyone other than the KGB he could have just walked out and pocketed the money, but the bad news is, they now owned him and he knew that and so did they!

"Mr Ivankov, this is a one time payment for a one time assignment, once you have successfully produced the results we require, a further payment will be made and your employment with us will cease". Cease....he hoped this was a ceasing of his verbal contract and not a deceasing of his own life?

Alexander asked what it was he had to do and at this point he was asked to follow Mr Andropov out of the room and up the long narrow corridor, with many rooms and doors running off of it.

Then swiftly, they made their way into a room, there were three other people inside, who appeared to be checking for listening devices or something in the room. They gave "the boss" the all clear and the conversation continued.

It transpired that yes, this was a KGB assignment and, in fact the KGB had sent agents to every single workshop Alexander hosted, to see if what he did could be replicated by the KGB. Their conclusion was he was too knowledgeable and too specialist in his field, that the KGB could not undertake his line of work themselves, they could only achieve the workshop type results by using Alexander, hence this is why he was here.

The KGB had a mole, someone that was leaking information they thought to the USA, someone that was spying on Russia for the USA.

The KGB had narrowed their final selection of potential double agents down to 6 agents. But, to continue any further they needed proof. The agents were too sharp and too well connected to be ousted by conventional methods, but the KGB needed to know exactly who was double crossing them in order to 'remove' them from service.

Wow that was a great little 'real world' assignment for Alexander, get this wrong and he could be signing the death warrant for an innocent person.

He was asked over a few days to come up with the process to eliminate the innocent parties from the equation and to be left with the one guilty individual.

After this initial meeting he was driven home, back to his apartment, where a car and driver were stationed permanently outside for 2 days and two nights while Alexander set about defining the process he would use.

Once complete he simply left home got into the car and arrived back at the KGB Headquarters.

He met again with Andropov who looked over his plan, approved it immediately and put it into action.

Alexander joined Mr Andropov in a large conference room, it was planned that Alexander would say nothing but purely observe the body language of the accused KGB agents. Six agents later joined the two in the conference room and the discussion began.

Alexander explained that for a body language expert, these were not the most ideal circumstances to be in, 6 agents, 1 of whom was guilty all summoned to headquarters. Instantly, they all show the signs of genuine nerves. It's funny these guys are out in the field and can control every emotion, yet a single call from the boss to come back for a 'little meeting' puts them into panic mode, to be honest they were almost physically shitting themselves.

They were all informed that there was a mole amongst the six of them; the 'Komitet' knew which one was the guilty party and they were given the chance to make their admission there and then. As they suspected nobody offered their confession and all six agents were escorted out of the room with flanked by two heavily armed officers, as per my plan they were to escorted to individual holding cells in the basement, where he was to continue his observations later.

It was around four and a half hours later that he visited just the doors of each cell. The cells inside had no windows, no natural light and just a single spy-hole each door connecting the outside world, with the very insides of the KGB's interrogation nerve centre. He watched each cell through that small spy-hole for two hours, noting every relevant body movement for my detailed analysis.

After over 12 hours straight observation he was beginning to tire, so the KGB put him up in a nearby hotel and he returned the following morning for one last round of observations. After only 4 hours, he returned with his result, consulted the boss and showed him his findings.

Overall all agents were showing signs of stress and nerves as was to be suspect. But after one night's sleep, one agent in particular from "cell 3" in Alexander's professional estimations was without doubt the culprit.

Andropov was amazed but curious, how could Alexander be so confident so it was explained.

During the observations all agents were showing signs of nervousness, as was to be suspected. Five of the agents began to show slightly less signs and were giving off fewer body signals of stress and tension. This was natural as five agents had nothing to worry about in the long term; one however had a great deal to worry about.

Chapter 2: How To Successfully Learn To

Read Body Language

You can quite clearly see, just in this one story alone of Alexander's, not only was he a fascinating man, but also extremely knowledgeable in his field.

How does a man become so confident, that he can state and make categorically a decision that will affect another person's life forever?

How does someone learn this skill and get it right every time and how could I learn this mysterious skill?

This was the question I asked him while at the barbeque with him in Cyprus. It was here that my training began my insight into how I could read people. This is where your training should begin too.

Alexander (or Alex as I was allowed to refer to him) asked me to do something while he continued cooking the meat (Souvla) on the barbeque.

"Close your eyes and look down to the floor, count to 2 open your eyes and then raise your head up and instantly make direct eye contact with my gaze."

"How many pieces of meat are on the skewer he asked?".

Which left me a little dumbfounded initially, I wanted to learn this mysterious art of body language and he is asking what he is cooking!

He explained in detail the following:

The art of being able to read someone or something is to lock away an image to take a snapshot of your surroundings and lock it away in your memory as a reference point.
Everyone takes photographs with a camera but actually some of the best photographs we have are those which are stored in our memory. If a fire occurred at your house and all of your holiday snaps were engulfed in the fire, you may not be able to physically replace them, but in your memory they are stored much more vividly than in real life.

So, he asked me to try it again.

17

I closed my eyes looked down to the ground, counted to 2 opened my eyes and then looked up at him. I knew, in fact I was confident that there were six pieces of meat on the skewer. He then asked......How many skewers are there on the barbeque? Whoops, I didn't see that coming and obviously I admitted defeat once again.

He said let's finish cooking and we will eat and retry the training after. We ate a lovely meal with salad, humus, barbequed pork Souvla and fresh Cypriot pitta breads, whilst consuming a couple of KEO beers too.

Then quite normally he cleared the table and he told me we would proceed with the test. He asked I do the same as before, which I did.

"What was on the table?", "Nothing you just cleared it?" I replied. "Correct" he chuckled you are doing very well.

Then he asked me to do the same again, but this time he had placed a bottle top from his bottle of beer at the top right hand corner of the table, which was the furthest away from me.

We continued again, until I could name his brand of cigarettes, which way round items were after he had moved them etc.

Don't get me wrong this took quite a long time to get right and only occupies just a few paragraphs of this book, but it is something you have to practice. Make snapshots around you and perhaps get someone to help you, to encourage and stimulate your mind to become a mobile digital camcorder.
What happens with practice is your subconscious mind will automatically create these images for you without you needing to trigger it. It will just happen, believe me.

The following day when I was invited into his home, we discussed the night previously and I told him how enlightened I was by his stories and practical tests. Guess what? He asked me to close my eyes again and do exactly as I had done the night before. When I opened my eyes he asked what newspaper do I read, how many photographs are above the fireplace, are they of children or adults and what colour shoes am I wearing. I only remembered the newspaper, but it goes to show just 24 hours later I was beginning to train my brain.

He explained it took him 3 months to master this, but within 1 millisecond (and not two seconds as I was working on), he had a complete breakdown on his surroundings, visually stored away and 'on tap' whenever and wherever he needed it.

During another visit or training session as I would like to refer to them as, he then said once you have mastered the 'static' visualisation, move onto to 'mobile' visualisations...people.

People as I found out are much more difficult, everyone has different hair colours, different hairstyles etc, but with practice it also becomes second nature to your subconscious mind to take and store that all important snapshot.

Try it, next time you visit a restaurant, who's at the table behind you, what are they wearing, what are they drinking, what are they eating? Start with the basics until you have a full visual profile every time you walk in somewhere or do anything.

Because to be successful at reading body language, you have just a microsecond to read people and your mind must be prepared and ready to take that snapshot without warning.

This technique is training your visual memory; we have three types of memory retention.

The visual memory is for storing visual impressions the emotional memory is where we store emotions and sensations and our main memory, is where we store our information in words.

Our main memory is used the most and therefore our visual memory is utilised the least, hence our need to 'train' it.

Chapter 3: How To Use Body Language To

Improve Your Life

It is no secret and by now you should be aware that body language exists all around us, every second of the day, anytime we come into contact with another person.

Contact as we have seen, doesn't have to be physical contact, but quite often it is and it's during this physical contact that we can use the power of body language wisely and controllably to our own advantage.

Let's imagine you are sat in front of you bank manager or business manager at your local bank. You have a great idea, a cunning business plan and now all you have to do is 'sell' the idea to them to secure their support or their investment in you.

Watch their face and read it carefully, you will see when they like your idea and when they don't like your idea. By reading them correctly, you can manipulate the conversation in your favour. When you can quite clearly read that they don't like something, you can reiterate what you are saying to them, change it or indeed completely steer the conversation in another direction.

Perhaps you have the chance of a promotion within your career. How many other candidates will go in armed with the knowledge of body language? They will be more concentrating on what they can do for the company in their new role and how many extra hours they are prepared to put into their newly gained promotion. Wouldn't it be so much easier to sit in that interview with your employer and just be you....you armed with the information and reading skills to determine that with a flicker of an eye, that twitch of an arm or the slightly downturned lip you can just be you and still win that deserved increase in salary.

In your social circle your friends cannot help but lie, in fact we all do. They may be minor lies but with you new socially adapt body language reading skills; you'll be able to tell straight away. This will make you a much stronger pinnacle of you own social circle, by weeding out the truth from the lies and knowing when to act and when not.

23

With body language you can seriously change your life. The skills in the rest of the book will not turn you into the next James Bond, Sherlock Holmes or Miss Marple. But, with practice you will be able to empower your life and change you life in ways that weren't ever previously possible.

But remember to be successful; you have to practice and practice and practice again to read these situations. Once Alexander had given me my knowledge it was up to me to make this knowledge my power. Which after many months of hard work and perseverance, I now have the power!

Chapter 4: Reading The Eyes

My first real training with Alexander was informative and initially fun. But it was obviously just the foundations of body language reading. But in these initial stages I quickly realised how much we 'miss' in our environment around us and by missing these little things we can completely misinterpret what is really going on around us.

One of the most efficient behavioural indicators to read on a person is their eyes.

The eyes are broken down into two logical categories for the purposes of reading.

The views – what the eyes are actually focusing on.

The movements – how the eyes are reacting and moving.

The Views

What you have to remember is as a trainee body language reader, the eyes are both accurate and dangerous to read.

Because imagine if you study a subject's eye movements for too long, over and above what a normal initial, casual encounter would be. Both your subject's eyes and your own eyes will be giving out mixed messages and you will give and receive totally the wrong information.

So it is important when trying to read the eyes not to look at your subject for too long and not to study them for too short a period, just try to always keep to a normal behavioural pattern, no matter how excited and eager you are to learn your new techniques.

If you stare for too long you will be giving off the impression that you wish to dominate your subject. Should your encounter be too short then you are showing fear or shame.

This will then change the message sent by your subject through their subconscious mind into completely the opposite of what and how they would normally react. It is like a wall that

26

we all put up to protect our personal space. Once this wall is built it will be impossible to read or trust any further body language signs given off by the subject and therefore you should not continue with this subject.

In the extreme when this happens, say when a subject is under questioning or perhaps in a pub and under the influence of alcohol, this need to defend their personal zone becomes immense and can lead to extreme physical aggression just to protect your unsuccessful attempts to decrypt their eye language.

Curiously enough, we know obviously that dogs are non verbal communicators and they also use the eye view to communicate. They can and do set their eyes based upon their feelings..happy, sad or mad. When two dogs have the same 'setting' e.g. mad and mad, this is when two dogs will fight. That's why when you have a dog on a leash and it sees another dog, if they both have their 'mad eyes' on they start barking at one another, before they are even close. They have read each other's doggy body language before even getting that close. So, keep this in mind and don't turn your subject into a Rottweiler!

Again I cannot stress enough through this entire book.

Practice, practice and practice!

The art to becoming successful at reading human behaviour and body language is that you never change your own behavioural patterns while you're doing it. This might sound a little contradictory when you want to control the situation you are trying to read. But in those initial first few seconds it is extremely important that you can read your subject and that it's not your subject subconsciously reading you. Once you have that initial information then you'll be much better placed to 'steer' your subject in a direction you want them to go in, with verbal communication or to have made your conclusions if they were telling the truth, happy to see you, busy or disinterested in you.

Remember the view and the movement should be read in isolation of one another.

The movement of the eyes is showing how and where the subject stores their information e.g. in the conscious or subconscious mind.

The single view gives us the most trustworthy and reliable information of what your subject is interested in and the strength of their interest.

Analysing the views

It is important to remember that we are referring to the way the eye is viewing, not how it moves, but more the direction of the eye's gaze.

Eyes wide open – dilated pupils - your subject is very interested in what they are currently hearing, you have their full attention and they are open to suggestion.

Eyes partly closed – partly dilated pupils - your subject shows they are sceptical, they will now check and monitor how the conversation progresses or the initial meeting develops and if they agree with the conversation or meeting. At this stage always try to change the direction of conversation or the meeting circumstances back to eyes wide open. If eyes stay the same, change conversation or stop conversation/meeting and come back to the subject when their eyes are wide open.

Eyes look upwards - sign of the subject's helplessness they are looking for help at a higher point in their mind.

Eyes down - sign of weakness and submissiveness, go forward with your conversation or meeting, use their concerns and fears to show them that what you are suggesting or commencing is the right thing to do.

Eyes looking beyond – the subject is aiming at a target in the future and is trying to visualise not what is there now or what you have suggested now, but something far away in the future. Don't make any further pressure as they are not interested right now.

Eyes lose sight temporarily to the side - subject is processing the information and is trying to store the information in their sub conscious mind but also wants to store it in their long term memory for easier reference. So give them a short natural break to process it for a second.

Eyes losing site for a long time - complete loss of interest in the conversation or meeting. You need to stop the conversation or meeting in a normal manner so as to still retain any chance of reopening this conversation or meeting in the future.

Real Life Example

Let's imagine you are going to apply for a new job or promotion.

You sit down excitedly in the evening to tell your spouse this wonderful news. However, as you begin the conversation with them you notice that their Eyes are looking beyond you (into the future).

The eyes are telling you that your spouse is looking into the future, so you need to react to this. Help them visualise something in the future and connect with the information you have already told them.

Something like with the increase in salary we will be able to buy that house next year that we have wanted for so long, the nice one with the large garden and the double garage and the fish pond (always be descriptive, paint a picture to aide their visualisation).

Your response from your spouse should be one of agreement Eyes Wide Open, now you can go proceed with their full approval and acceptance.

In this short example you can see how you are able to steer the conversation in your favour, should the eyes be telling you something different, then you have to act and adapt accordingly.

The Movements

Movement of the eyes are far more difficult to interpret, but all form a general pattern to be able to read your subjects.
It is important that you first understand and can instantly detect what is a general eye movement, say through tiredness or dry eyes and what is just a movement, which is a direct

response to your conversation or indeed actions.

It is also important that you realise we are discussing only the single and isolated movements of the eyes and their interpretation as when these movements are combined with other body language signals, they can again mean something entirely different.

So, it is very important to learn the movements well and then to learn how these movements are effected with additional gestures.

Analysing the movements

Eye movements are almost always created when we process thoughts, you cannot control it, this just happens naturally in all of us.

In this chapter we will show the differences between the movement "up", "down" and "left to right" or "right to left".

Eyes moving up – generally means your subject thinks in pictures and sketches, they are the visual and creative.

Eyes moving left to right or right to left – the person is putting the information they have heard in their long term memory. They are the acoustic type responding to sound and not visuals.

Eyes moving down – the person is attaching emotions and feelings to your information. They are emotional so talk emotions.

When you can understand these simple movements and instantly recognise them, you will know how to talk to your subject, in pictures, with logic or with just emotions.

How your subject is receiving and processing your information is also extremely important.

To detect where this information is being stored you must again study for the movments:-

Eyes move to their right or your left they are creating in their mind something that hasn't

34

happened yet. So right at this moment they are going to tell or are telling you something they have just thought of or made up, perhaps they are lying to you.

Eyes move to their left or your right – they are trying to find information in their mind from the past, they are trying to relate the information you are giving them with a prior personal experience.

Eyes move to their right and down or your left and down – they are trying to put the information received in the emotional level of their mind, so you must be more emotional.

Eyes move to their left and down or your down and right - they are having an inner conversation with themselves, they are discussing what they are hearing with themselves

Using just these reading techniques alone we can tell if the information is new to them or not. Is it emotional enough for them or not. We can then use this power to gain further acceptance in the information we are delivering to them.

But beware this is the case only for a right handed person!

If your subject is left handed, then everything is reversed, so it is important to read all aspects of the body language before making your assumptions.

Real Life Example

For this example try out what you have learned so far in real life.

Ask your spouse or a friend to help.

You are going to ask them 5 questions (which you must prepare) and from the questions at least one them, they must tell a lie.

Keep trying this with different friends until you get it correct every time.

Eyebrows

Whilst I was making my initial notes with Alexander, he told me it is extremely important to know absolutely everything the body tells us, to make a note of every single 'tell' and to remember, study it and continue to practice it.

You may now know how to read the body language of the Eyes, but it is important not to lose sight (excuse the pun) of the rest of the entire body, because by encompassing all the skills we now know, you will get a much fuller idea of your subjects.

Although not deserved of its own entire chapter, it would be a massive mistake not to take into account the signs given by the Eyebrows. The eyebrows alone will give us a huge insight into how we are interpreted socially, how our subjects see us in non-verbal communication.

Eyebrow movements are involuntary microsecond movements that are shown and are impossible to hide. We kind of forget about our eyebrows as they are stuck up there on our foreheads and we forget that they are one of the most prominent features that people can see and often from quite a distance too.

This is one of the reflexes that we inherited from our Stone Age ancestors, it is one that we use daily and interpret subconsciously to determine the real truth behind someone's expressions. Using these eyebrow movements combined with other movements we can literally begin to read people like a book.

When someone raises their eyebrows for a millisecond, their field of vision and peripheral vision is temporarily enlarged and their pupils will dilate.

At this moment, what that person is saying to you is 'I'm interested in what you have to say, tell me more, give me more information...now'. They are captive and should their eyes then move down, you have them in a submissive, captive state. If this is your next date then you have made a very good first impression

Try it on your friends and acquaintances, do it when someone is watching you from the corner of their eye. Just flick your eyebrows up for a millisecond and see how long it takes them to engage in conversation with you.

Eyebrows are one of the best indicators to show when someone is angry or dislikes something or someone.

Your face is actually supported by your eyebrows; they are like a wooden or steel support beam running across the bottom of your forehead holding the rest of your face in place.

So, when those beams 'give in', an upward, downwards or sideways direction, you can be sure that you're whole face shows the movement too.

Just like you can see from a distance if a structure is wonky or lopsided, you can spot instantly from a distance if someone is unhappy or potentially aggressive towards you.

Eyebrows show what the eyes cannot, the eyes will show if someone likes or dislikes what we are saying or if they are emotional about it or not. The eyebrows show if they agree or disagree or are surprised by what we are saying.

If a person makes a split second movement of their eyebrows in an upwards direction, almost like a twitch, then they are really surprised about what you are saying.

The opposite is true when the eyebrows are making a much slower and more gradual movement upwards. This then means the person is trying to decide with the knowledge they have, if what you are saying is true or false.
If they were then to combine this with a slight almost unnoticeable upward movement of the head, they have discovered that they don't like what you are saying and possibly feel you are being untruthful or non-factual.

Imagine giving your next speech about your company, product or thesis to a small group of people.
You have the patter down expertly and hope to give the presentation of your life, look around the room and you will instantly be able to decipher your audience's reaction, if the are all twitching their eyebrows upwards you are on a winner, if not then you need to read them again and adjust your speech delivery accordingly.

One of the first cases Alexander was involved in for the KGB was also one of his most difficult. He received a call to take part in a very intense interview and was collected from his apartment as usual and ferried to the KGB headquarters basement.

He was greeted by two KGB officers and asked to proceed to the viewing room with them.

The viewing room was a small dimly lit room adjacent to an interrogation cell. On the left hand side of the room was a pane of dark glass about 8 feet long and 6 feet high and the room was not that much longer or wider. At first he was shocked to be able to see into the interrogation room.

Alexander Ivankov was a private man, sure he was good at what he did, but he did not really want everyone else knowing he was 'assisting' the KGB. He told the officers he was not comfortable to be in this room and then the officer explained the room was soundproof and that they were stood behind a one way mirror, nobody inside the interrogation cell could see through this mirror. Alexander felt very stupid now, of course this is what the

41

glass was, he had seen rooms just like it on television hundreds of times, but never even for a second thought he would ever be stood this side of one.

One of the officers left the viewing room and shortly after the same officer entered the interrogation room with another man and they sat opposite each other. Inside the viewing room everything could be heard and it became clear that this other man was a 'suspect' for something that had happened which affected the KGB.

Alex began to make notes, over three hours worth of notes to be precise. He was monitoring the body language of the 'suspect' and what was most curious for him, was the fact that the suspect was giving off no 'guilty' signals whatsoever.

When asked a question, the suspect gave a brief pause then replied, in a cool, calm and collected manner and then proceeded to answer the next line of interrogation.

It was during these 3 hours that Alex thought to himself that perhaps all his years of behaviour and body language studies had finally come unravelled, perhaps there was times when we could not read a person and unfortunately this might be one of them.

This subject was not giving away a single sign by which he could be successfully become accused, not even an increase of blood pressure or a slight twitch anywhere.

After 3 hours the interviewer and suspect were given a break and after just 30 minutes the interview or interrogation recommenced. Alex continued to observe from the viewing room with the other KGB officer.

After 2 hours he was still dumbfounded, here was someone he just couldn't decipher. How could he go back to 'the boss' and say sorry I have nothing that would surely be the end of his time with the KGB and possibly worse?

Then he had an idea, he wrote something down on a piece of paper, folded it in half and gave it to the officer beside him to take to the interviewer. Which, he then observed happening through the mirror and the messenger then left the cell and returned to the viewing room and stood next to Alex.

Alex then asked the officer to wait 5 minutes and to return to the interrogation cell and pretend to whisper something in the ear of the interviewing officer. Sure enough as requested this happened.

Then 20 minutes later the interviewer told the suspect that a partial fingerprint had been found on the weapon and as the suspect had obviously been very truthful with him he was keen to eliminate him from their enquiries and to let him return home. He informed the suspect he was going to check the partial print against their records and it would not take long and then he could be released. The interviewer left slamming the heavy cell door behind him.

Just 15 minutes later the interviewer returned, handcuffed the subject and told him he hoped he could remember what his family looked like, as it would be a long time before he would ever see them again and that he was off to Siberia (Which was an infamous place used by the KGB to 'discard' their problems!).

Alex was driven home and received a telephone call, one which he was initially dreading, but instead it was one to congratulate him on his work!

Because, there was no partial fingerprint and the interviewer did not go out to check the fingerprint records!

The message Alex wrote said the following:

"I cannot read the subject, so we have to try a different approach. Please acknowledge the officer when he enters the room, listen to his 'pretend' whispers and say the following 20 minutes later."
The rest we know.

But there were no fingerprints, yet Alexander correctly identified the subject's guilt. How could this be?

As soon as the interviewer told the subject this news, the subject's eyebrows flickered upwards for just a short second. Showing the subject was surprised. If he were 'innocent' then the reaction should have been one of concern or worry not of surprise. The subject also instantly began to stare past the interviewer e.g. to think about the future, what would happen to him once the truth was revealed. Also in the 15 minutes that the interviewer was out of the cell, 'checking the records'. The suspect was becoming increasingly anxious, his blood pressure was obviously raised, which could be seen by a redness under his skin and also his fingers were gripping tightly to his thighs a sure sign that this was their man.

So Alex explained, this was really a difficult subject to read and most people would have given up and gone home, but you have to try different techniques to begin to receive signals from people. It doesn't always happen instantly and his perseverance paid off in the end.

Chapter 5: Reading The Face

After we have looked at the eyes and eyebrows in isolation, it is now only logical that we should look at the rest of the head and face and how it relates to body language.

Just like the eyes, the face gives not only its own signals, but when combined with other signals from the face or other areas of the face or body it can read as something completely different.

So it's important like we have said previously not only to be able to 'read' these signs, but to correctly interpret both their individual and combined meanings in relation to our body language.

Also it's extremely important to read the whole face, eyes, eyebrows and muscle movements to gain the absolute facts about what your subject is telling you.

The Face is split into four main areas, whereby each area tells us something in body language terms.

In general we can divide the head into:

The whole head and how it is held.

The forehead.

The nose and the area around the nose.

The mouth and the area around the mouth.

On first view it would seem almost unlikely, but you like me might be surprised to learn that my 'mentor' Alexander told me that the head is one of the most interesting parts of body language.
But actually as I learnt it is true and something which I now totally agree with.
Even the smallest nod or subconscious movement of the head can show you how your subject is receiving your conversation.

You can experience this first-hand, choose one of the countless TV chat shows or political conferences and watch it with the sound off.

Trying looking only at the heads and you will be surprised what you can glean from these TV show's. Actually, this is great way to learn body language. One way I found which was invaluable to me, was to record the show without watching it. Watch the recording back a few times with no sound and then play it with sound and see how right I interpreted the signs I saw.

When you carry out this experiment you will soon realise that there are only a few movements of the head that signal a reply.

A slow nod gives the signal that the listener is paying attention to the speaker and respects what the speaker is saying.

A fast brief repetitive nod is showing that that the listener is agreeing with what the speaker is saying, giving it their own personal nod of approval.

A fast repetitive, but more prolonged repetition of nods shows that the listener is agreeing, but is more anxious for the speaker

49

to finish speaking, so that the listener can talk and give their own point of view on the subject.

The position of the head does not only show how and what someone thinks or how that information is being processed, but also the position of the head is able to manipulate the audience.
It gives us information in the first instance about the emotions, but it is also able to awake emotions from others.

A head which is upright shows us arrogance a feeling that the person is better than their opposites and this will not awake positive actions from their opposites.

A head drooping downwards show us that a person is voluntarily bowing down to us, almost submissive.
But if their eyes remain in contact with us, while the head is still downwards then this is a sign of defiance. This awakes in the opposite that you were too strong with them or you have exceeded their point of 'fairness' or good behaviour.

When the head is titled in a sideways direction, it is not so easy to interpret and we have to be very careful when trying to read a person as you will see now.

Because a head which is titled, gives us the view to their carotid artery the visible artery in the neck. Which in turn shows us their vulnerability, their sensitve side, which is open for attack. This shows they totally trust, but is expecting us to show trust in return. So we can use this to advantage, when you receive this signal then you should naturally reciprocate by slightly tilting our own head and therefore showing we are giving them our trust and from here we are communicating directly with their emotions.

If we think about this in everyday life, next time you need to borrow something from a friend or neighbour, just approach them and talk to them in a soft tone of voice and while asking expose your vulnerability by tilting you head slight and expose your vulnerable neck artery, you will be surprised at the results.
But do not fall into the trap that many men fall into....Women know about this body language, subconsciously as soon as you meet

a woman in a bar or disco, instinctively when they are getting on well with you, they will tilt their heads almost offering their vulnerability to you, but it may get them many drinks and lots of attention for the evening, but at the end of the night you will only receive a polite 'good bye'!

Be careful about this 'trap', it is the most dangerous trap to fall into and happens everyday to every man.

Just try it yourself at random and see just with this body language sign alone how different the world and people around you will become.

Remember when you try this to tilt your head to the right as this is you emotional side, if you tilt it to the left this is your logical side and will show that you trust in what you have just heard.

The Forehead

An area of the face which is much easier to read than the eyes is the forehead. Because, it is easy to see and extremely difficult to disguise what it is saying. Subconsciously we see it and read it automatically. The art of reading it, is to no longer see it subconsciously and without thinking, but to analyse it and interpret it manually.

It is also the more difficult to describe in words, so I hope you can absorb and understand the following interpretations.

When the forehead is slightly raised, creating a small horizontal fold across it, you're your subject is trying to visualise the information you are presenting them and are converting it to a picture to store in their memory for later use.

However, when the forehead produces a vertical fold, just above the nose, you're subject is struggling to understand you and is finding it extremely difficult and an uphill battle to comprehend what you are saying.

The worst signal you can receive is when the forehead drops, just above the eyebrows; your subject without any doubt is now angry and critical. This is extremely negative and dangerous body language a sign which means you are very wrong in what you have just said or done and you're subject will almost certainly follow your actions with verbal or physical aggression towards you.

The Nose

The nose is by far the easiest bodily function to read. The nose knows only one subconscious reflex that you need to learn and understand.

For a short second the nose will sometimes twitch, this shows you that your subject has a general dissatisfaction with the current situation you are either discussing or showing to them.

A classic example of this is when you take someone out for a meal to a restaurant.
When you are taken to your table to be seated, when you gesture, or pull out the chair for the other person to sit on, if they make this twitch of the nose, then it means that they do not want to sit at that particular chair, they are subconsciously uncomfortable with the choice you have made for them and it would be a much better option to offer them a different seat or perhaps another table?

If however, your dinner partner makes this twitch as you enter the restaurant, prior to being seated then it means they are uncomfortable with either the whole restaurant or just the idea of dining with you.

I wish that all waiters and waitresses were taught this as part of their job description, so as to stop giving me the worst table in the restaurant every time!

The Mouth

A much more interesting region for body language is the mouth and the area around it.

It should be a region that you already know the basics about. When someone smiles, they are happy and the corners of their mouth and lips are upturned and when their mouth and lips drop in the opposite direction they are sad.

These are not the only things that we can read from the movements of the mouth.

When someone loses the control of their lips and the mouth becomes slightly open, the subject is surprised and overwhelmed by what you are saying or doing.

In real life when you see this happen, directly after the subject will quickly close the mouth again and regain control of their lips once more, because subconsciously they have just realised what they did.

The complete opposite motion when your subject keeps their lips and mouth firmly pressed together and their jaws are also held together tight, means the subject doesn't want to speak, be part of or take anything from your information. Although they have considered your information, they are not prepared to change their own view. The subject's ego will not be ruined by you trying to change their mind or their beliefs, they are not going to adjust their disposition, just for your facts, however truthful or plausible they may be.

In reality the subject is concluding that their meaning or version of the information is the truth and that there is no way whatsoever that they could be wrong.

However, they are emotionally attached or involved in your actions and they are not uninterested in what you are doing, but simply they don't want to partake at this particular moment as they cannot afford to be proved wrong and damage their ego.

You will observe this very often when people are talking about one common thing which has no true right or wrong.

A classic example is when you get two or three people together from different religious beliefs, talking about religion and god. In their eyes and their religion, their god is the only one and correct one and they will not be told otherwise.

But the mouth can also show us much, much more.

Downturned as we know is unhappy and negative emotionally. Upturned is happy.

But upturned in a less natural smile, almost a grimace can be interpreted as a fake smile, it's not from the heart or soul, but instead one of either mockery or impatience.

A slightly upturned mouth on one side is a show of disgust. Add to this wide open eyes and your subject is showing you their rage.

Sometimes, it is what you don't see from the mouth movements that can give away the most secrets. It now makes me laugh when people put their hand up to their mouth to conceal something they are saying, or when they lean across to someone else and put their hand up to mask what they are telling that person. Just look at the rest of the body language they are shouting out and you will know 70% of what was just said within what they thought was the safe confounds of their own palm.

The face is a region of our bodies which is always visible during conversation.

But to use body language successfully it is necessary that you thoroughly study and know the combination of all these areas to completely ascertain the full picture, because perhaps what the eye doesn't tell you, the head might and what the lips can't tell you the forehead might.

This body language is not only necessary for reading other people successfully, when you have a conversational goal, you will need to control and develop your own indicators and micro movements, that you give out to your subjects so as to fully and successfully achieve your target.

Most major corporations have a human resources (HR) department and most of these HR personnel have fully studied body language reading and will be reading you to see if you are a suitable mix for their employer, therefore it is so important that you can not only read but also be read exactly as you wish.

Also never forget that what is subconsciously sent can also be subconsciously received, it is important further still that you learn to control and nurture your subconscious actions.

Quite often when we are feeling down, it can actually be that we have subconsciously stored something away, without even realising and it has changed our own mood!

Alex told me one night that body language is really the only language we need to remember, it is the oldest and most honest language a human can use. In the development of the verbal language the words are constantly filling our subconscious minds, now we have to cast these aside to make room for the unspoken language...body language.

Now that you understand how you can begin to read a person just using the face and understand how powerful this is. You must also understand that this really only occurs during or at the commencement of a conversation.

Therefore, we must learn about the rest of the body, which will give us a much clearer idea of how our subject is going to receive us.

Because reading a face is easy to do when you are up close and personal with your subject, but from 20 metres away it is impossible to make an accurate reading.

When a pilot lands a plane in the fog, it is possible to do and they do it many thousands of times in their career. But sometimes there is an error of judgement which can lead to an accident or even is some cases fatalities.

Reading just the face from a distance can lead us into the same kind of difficulties which although detrimental to what we are trying to achieve, hopefully will never be as catastrophic.

It is always much better to make a 'judgement call' with a clear view of your subject, ask any pilot!

Chapter 6: Posture, Special Features And

Protection Zones

Before we breakdown the rest of the body parts and the language that they communicate to us, it is important to study exactly what the body overall is trying to tell us.

Outside of every human we have invisible zones, which are called 'distance zones'.

These are like invisible circles around us, each a different radius around our body and each incremental zone is known as collectively as a distance zone.

The difference between these distance zones decide in advance how comfortable we will feel in a conversation or how uncomfortable we will feel with these conversations and even more importantly how we will react, when someone holds a conversation within these zones or approaches our different zones.

These zones will give us a completely different picture of a conversation, than perhaps we wanted or expected.

You can use these zones to increase your chances of getting the result you need. An invasion in to a subjects distance zone can diffuse conflicts or indeed can create conflicts just by invading those very same zones.

So, remember you can use these zones to get the reaction you want.

Everyone has the desire for space, their own 'personal' space. A desire that is dependent on different cultural signs, but all the time this desire is always there.

Adequate control of our personal distance zones enables us to prepare to defend a zone or let someone into as zone as we desire.

An invasion of our zone means we don't have enough space and you will know the saying "I don't have enough space to breath", this is when someone feels that their space has been invaded.

Everything plays out around our natural distance zone our "comfort zone" but occasionally things do breach out most personal distance zone (the zone closest to us). We are always subconsciously aware and protective of this and when out zone is breached we act accordingly; this can be in many ways for instance aggressively, acceptingly or even lovingly.

Imagine you are sitting at your desk and you share your desk with another work colleague.

Subconsciously without thinking, you will arrange your half of the desk as you want it. It is like there is an imaginary line, defining the border between your personal space and your work colleague's personal space.

If you colleague also adopts this method of working, you are immediately comfortable and can work well with this arrangement.

However, if a new work colleague shares your desk and they begin to move paperwork or anything else over your imaginary border, you will begin to feel very uncomfortable and begin to possibly make mistakes and your productivity will lessen as you concentration will be more focused on the invasion of your distance zone.

These distance zones for Europe and America can be categorised into 4 unique zones, each having their own characteristics.

The intimate zone, the personal zone, social zone and the public zone.

The intimate zone is an imaginary invisible circle, which projects at a maximum radius of 40 cm around you. In this circle, you will let only in the true sense of the word "close" people in, for instance your spouse, certain members of your family and very close acquaintances.

The personal zone, is an invisible circle, which has a maximum radius of 40 cm – 1m 50cm around you. This is a circle that you let in colleagues and acquaintances. This circle is probably the most acceptable and closest you will let most people breach, for instance if you go out to the cinema or theatre, it will be acceptable for people to come into this zone as you have already agreed mentally to take this zone out into the public and to let people come in and out of this zone, for the sake of a 'nice time out'. This zone is also the closet zone you will feel comfortable holding day to day conversations in.

Much further away is the social zone 1m 50 – 4m. This zone is reserved for less important things. A good example of this could be when you are expecting someone to your home, for instance a Gardner, pool boy or plumber. Generally, you would open your front door, step back let them through to carry on their duties and keep an observational distance away from them while they worked.

This is the same for instance if you were waiting in a hotel lobby for someone, nothing would phase you by being in this zone, it is only when say the hotel porter comes closer than this zone to tell you your room is ready, that your zonal protection would kick in and initiate a response.

Last but not least is your public zone which is generally everything 4m and further. This is a zone that has very little meaning or consequences to you and actually you have very little awareness of it. Anyone trying to communicate with you in this zone may as well be shouting from the top of Mount Everest. It is only when people come closer from this zone that we begin to subconsciously 'raise our guard'.

Chapter 7: Reading The Neck, Back And

Shoulders

The Shoulders

The shoulders like the neck and face are always visible. The first time you see or meet someone, you can see immediately their neck or shoulders, often from a distance.

The shoulders in relation to readings of body language from the face are an extremely trustworthy sign for us to read about any subject and have basically two signals. The two signals show us the actual mood of the subject.

So, it is important that we learn and instantly recognise the two important body language signs.

If a person's shoulders are dropped or drooped, it shows us they are generally demotivated, perhaps under pressure in their work life, under financial pressure or have pressures in their relationship or personal life.

Dropped shoulders show that whatever the pressure is, the person had gone past the point and over the border of what they can psychologically cope with.

If a person's shoulders are horizontally straight then this shows they are confident and able to manage everything life throws at them. They are motivated and saying 'yes' to life.

Try an experiment at home which has some interesting results.

Stand in front of a full length mirror and make your whole body relaxed and generally lethargic. By doing this, note that your shoulders should be dropped and your overall look will be relaxed and uninterested.

After 1 minute of standing like this say to yourself out loud "I am confident, I am happy, I am satisfied and I am able to do anything I want and succeed".

Did you believe what you just said? I bet you didn't! Your body language is telling your brain that what you have just said is unbelievable.

Now change your posture bring your shoulders up, stand tall and proud and after 1 minute say the same thing again out loud "I am confident, I am happy, I am satisfied and I am able to do anything I want and succeed".

What a difference! Now it is not only believable but also you feel it.

So it is important to remember this and how much difference it makes when you are in communication with someone or they are with you. Just such a small change in the posture of your shoulders, can show a huge amount of information.

Have you ever been to a job interview and halfway through felt that it wasn't going your way? If you cast you mind back, I would like to bet that you dropped your shoulders. If you hadn't then you might have got that job as the interviewer wouldn't have seen that you get despondent quickly!

There is a third signal that the shoulders give and that is when they are raised in the opposite direction to when they are dropped for example raised above their normal horizontal line.

This means the subject has fear or is fearful, what the shoulders are trying to do is actually shroud and protect the neck and face. If you think about the times when you have had a sudden surprise like someone jumping out at you or perhaps a dog barking, your shoulders rise up. It is this reaction that we are referring to here, the one of fear.

The Back

When the back is rounded or hunched and the shoulders are then consequently dropped it shows that your subject is finding everything hard to follow or accept.

They are subconsciously fighting against what you are saying or indeed the body language you are portraying to them. They are actually facing up to what you have just said, but in the same turn are fighting against it too!

Alexander's office was based at the start of a long corridor in the KGB's headquarters. From his window in his office he could see straight to the end of this long corridor some thirty metres long. There were a few offices off of the corridor and one solitary door at the end of it.

This door lead to the office of the internal affairs officer. The corridor was known as 'the corridor of truth' between Alex and the officer.

On the same month every year, the KGB would have an internal affairs review of all its agents. This review was determine those agents who were still able to perform and their commitment levels to the secret service. It wasn't uncommon for agents of all secret services to stray across a couple of agencies and become double agents, playing for both sides, but in the KGB it was critical to 'weed' them out.

To do this became quite a simple task as it turned out for Alexander.

He would sit in his office and watch as each agent was called to the review room. As soon as the agent began the long walk, Alex studied his posture. Was the agents back hunched? Were their shoulders drooped? Using this and a combination of body language signs you have already learned in this book, he would make a call to the internal affairs officer, before the agent even reached the room! It was kind of a 'tip off' as to what Alex perceived the agent to be like, under pressure, unable to cope, uninterested, all the signs that an agent might be ready to leave the service or be playing for the other side.

It was a basic system, but one which worked and kept the KGB ahead of its agents. Every time this review came around each year, the agents would all get 'twitchy' as they knew what had happened to agents before them that had got 'caught out'. Like we already know, when people are under pressure they unwittingly give away the slightest details that could showcase their 'guilt' and what better place to view this pressure, where they think they aren't being watched!

When reading body language signals of the shoulders, it is important to also watch the torso, the part of the body from the chest to the stomach and the side from underneath the armpits down to the side of the stomach.

But be careful, the torso is only a secondary indicator and should never be read on its own and only in conjunction with other signs.

When a subjects torso is bent slightly forward directly in front of them, even when they are walking or moving it shows they are wanting and willing to get closer to you, to form a relationship or engage in conversation with you.
However is their eyes are slightly squinted and their forehead is showing a frown, then beware as they are likely to physically attack you.

If a subjects torso is in the opposite direction, leaning back, even when they are moving then subconsciously they on 'on the run', escaping from a conversation, situation or someone. If it is during a conversation then they are mentally withdrawing from the conversation and have lost interest in whatever is being said and have closed their mind totally.

If you think about a politician or a person giving a speech on television at the start of the speech they will generally lean forward, their torso bent forward and they will conduct most of the speech in this way. At the end of the speech you will notice their whole body language switch, they will bend backwards. It's a signal subconsciously that this is the end of the speech. Kind of like the last full stop on the last chapter of a book.

If a subject has the torso bent forward and they have their hands behind their back, they are interested in what you have to say and the information you are providing, but they have also fear and apprehensions.
At this point you should also be reading the head, forehead and eyes to see what level of interest there is and how you could allay their fears.

As you can see the torso really is a secondary indicator and as the book progresses you will see it is more and more important to read all the signs from all the parts of the body, before you begin to interpret what a subject is subconsciously telling you.

The final and worse indicator the torso can give is if someone is in a discussion with you and their head and eyes are directed at you but the torso is turned to the side, it shows they are really interested in what you are saying, but they don't like you!

At this point you either have to change your body language and character or give up trying at this point, because although the subject is retaining the information you are offering, they will not trust it or act upon it as they don't like you and therefore don't trust you.

Chapter 8: Reading The Hands, Arms And

Fingers

Reading the shoulders and torso separately from the rest of the body is fairly easy and it will not take you long to remember instantly what people are telling you subconsciously. It was probably at this stage in my research that I began to find a real fascination in reading body language and thought that I knew most of it.

However, then came the hands, arms and fingers. If you think right now, without knowing what anything actually means how many different movements there are in these joints alone, there are thousands of combinations and interpretations that we could think of.

It was at this stage that I realised, I still had a long way to go to master the subject of reading body language like Alexander, but as you will find it makes it so much more worthwhile once you are armed with these secrets, your work life and social life will develop a whole new meaning and you will find yourself so much more confident in many situations.

It is important therefore to practice and practice the arms, hands and fingers reading along with what you already know.

Like we did with the face we will also spilt this into logical sections so it is easier to comprehend and study in your leisure.

Before we look in detail about the individual movements, it is important that we take a view of the general movements that give the overall strengths to this part of body language delivery and reading.

A very good example is political campaigns and speeches. If you watch a politician when they are delivering their speeches they use arm and hand movements a great deal. This is no accident; they are specially trained in how to deliver speeches and how to use their body to subconsciously gain an advantage over their audience and competing parties.

This kind of body language is used as an extremely effective instrument to gain a synergy with their voters and potential voters.

One of the most common movements you will see is when the speaker shows the back of their arm and hand and raises it from a level position, often with a clenched fist. Once it is raised they open their hand as though they are grabbing an apple from a tree high above them.

Subconsciously they are taking the audience with them during their speech, the audience is being asked to be powerful and to grasp the opportunity that the politician is talking about.

When you see the politician with a flat palm almost banging it in a downward motion, sometimes making actual contact with a podium or desk, then they are normally dissecting the policies and plans of competing parties, subconsciously they are asking you to agree and by using this motion it is locking in the negative dialect with almost a non-verbal 'full stop', which in turn is locking in bight sized negative information about the competing parties into your brain.

Try this next time you are talking to someone.

When you have something positive to say about something as you say it reach up in to the air and grab that 'apple' from the tree. It will make the person you are talking to believe it is a wonderful opportunity.

Then during the conversation when you have something negative to say about something for instance 'it is just too expensive', use your hand to bang downwards and affirm its negativity.

You'll be extremely surprised how quickly you can get your points across and how well they are received.

But as we know, body language isn't just for politicians, it is actually the perfect instrument of manipulation that everyone can and does use.

Let us start with something general that everyone knows and uses on a daily basis, the handshake. The saying 'first impressions count' is never more true than when we give or receive a handshake. Because, it is the very first from of bodily contact with a conversational partner, it is also the first sign of body language that you can manipulate to gain your advantage.

So, we will first take a look at what happens when you receive a handshake and how either you or the person you are greeting will interpret this first vital subconscious coming together.

The first thing you would quite naturally do when you are greeting someone is raise your arm and hand up in readiness to receive a handshake.

One possibility is your hand and outwardly affectionate gesture is ignored and your reaction to this will make you feel alone and displaced.

However, if you do receive a handshake, but one that is loose, without any effort or feeling and a bit like a 'wet rag', you will know instantly that this person has low self-esteem and has very little belief and confidence in themselves, if it was someone that was previously perceived to be a figure of 'power' and 'strength' then this handshake shows their truer side and now you know they aren't quite as powerful as you once thought.

The opposite is true when you receive a handshake that is strong, so strong that it almost hurts. You are now being told by the giver of that handshake that they are openly powerful and know and control their own destiny and line and will not be stopped or hampered by anyone or anything, least of all their meeting with you.

That last type of handshake is when you receive a handshake that just shakes your fingers and doesn't grasp your whole hand at all. This is a sign of mistrust; someone that is living a lie has self-doubts and is likely to lie to you in the not so distant future.

When you deliver a handshake it is important to give a handshake that is neither to strong and not too weak. This type of handshake shows the receiver, you believe in yourself are optimistic and importantly not a threat by being too strong and not too weak so that they will become uninterested by you.

To achieve this handshake you should deliver your arm straight out in front of you, don't come downwards or upwards in your deliver just directly horizontally. When you engage with the receivers hand you hand should slide up until you thumb joints are touching theirs and the physical grasp should be halfway between weak and strong.

One last tip on giving the perfect handshake is if it is important e.g. formal for business or perhaps a job, run you hand under warm water first and then dry it. This removes all the sweat from it and makes it the perfect temperature for the perfect delivery, it also gives an extremely positive signal to the receiver, and they don't remember you as the one with cold hands or sweating hands, just the one with a very good and optimistic handshake.

Never forget the power of the handshake, it is the very first contact and impression that you make with an individual and one that they remember the first.

But as we know, it is not the only method of body language that we use and you have to encompass everything to make the very first liaison the most successful one.

It is therefore critical that you practice reading the signs and practice delivering the right signs over and over again.

Unfortunately, the hands are one part of the body that can often be hidden and impossible to read.

Many years ago it was unthinkable and a sign of disrespect to hold a conversation while your hands were in your pockets. This seems to have changed like many traditions in modern day, someone having their hands in their pockets now can often be read as someone that is comfortable and leisurely in their manner, but could also be construed as a lazy individual, because they cannot be bothered to remove their hands and address someone in a more formal and polite manner.

Don't ever fall into this trap that it is socially acceptable to keep your hand or hands in your pockets while talking to people. You can trigger many more emotions and deliver more feeling in any speech you deliver by using your arms and hands.

Think about the news you see on television every day. There sits a news anchor-man or woman and you never see them using their hands, sometimes at most they might have a pen in their hand but that is all. They are simply there to deliver the news, not emotions. It is up to you then to interpret the news you are watching and listening to and make your own emotions. Also the news is delivered like this to not show any bias or favouritism to any particular feature.

The opposite is true when you look at breakfast television news, where the whole program is often hosted on a sofa with various guest appearances, intertwined with condensed news discussions or announcements which are made by the presenters on the sofas.

On this type of show, you will see much more use of body language during the chats, news and discussion. Which is why these types of television programs are so popular, because they are delivered subconsciously with lots more emotion.

A spokesperson that uses their arms and hands during their speech awakes emotions and reactions, but a speaker that uses nothing and no actions will be quickly and easy forgotten. You will always remember the content and the speaker that is more animated and emotional.

Hands and arms are also a great body language signal to read from afar. You can watch two people having a discussion from a distance and without hearing a single word you can quickly and easily determine if they are angry or happy, powerful or submissive and aggressive or defensive.

The handshake is the only active and physical body language signal that we can give and control. We have to make physical and real contact with our subject to be able to deliver or read the body language.
All other signals are passive and do not require us to be physically in contact with our subject to read or deliver them.

To be correctly informed about the body language signals given by the hands we also need to look at the fingers.

Although the fingers aren't a complete picture, they will help in an overall reading and each finger is able to project a different and individual message of its own.

So we will now examine what each finger and combination of finger movements are trying to tell us.

Our thumbs are a general sign for power and force. It is amazing that it is a part of the body that we often give little thought or consideration for, yet it is one of the most utilised parts of our body.

You can make a little experiment, try not using your thumb got the next two hours...I give you about 20 minutes before you give in and succumb to the temptation to open a bottle, type on your keyboard or lock your door!

When you see someone you are in conversation with twitching their thumb, rasping against their fingers in a stroking fashion, it is a big clue that your subject has only their self-interests at heart and egoism. It is kind of a sign of impatience; they can't wait until you are finished or possibly are on the verge of interrupting you, to get their own point across to gain something from you or to lay down something that is of benefit to them.

It is important to remember this is a reaction and not an action and therefore is an excellent signal to read.

Also once the subject has made this reaction, you will know that anything they then begin to speak about is about them, for their own self-importance, gain and egoism.

Chapter 9: The Russian Revolution And The

Formation Of The Cheka

Vladimir Lenin's plan for a Russian Civil War received a catalyst from a strange place. In September of 1915, Tsar Nicholas II dismissed his generals on the Eastern Front during World War I and took over military command himself. Thus, as the number of battles lost grew, his reputation and popularity among the people fell. By 1917, it was clear that the Russian Army would never be able to sustain further involvement in the war, having already lost almost 8 million soldiers to death, injury and capture. With that, the Russian people began to cry out against the privations of the war. Factory workers staged strikes for higher wages to pay the ever inflating cost of food for their families. At the same time, people in Petrograd rioted in the streets, vandalizing shops and demanding food that the government simply did not have.

Lenin

Had he been wiser, Nicholas might have appealed to the people, or met with the Duma to work out some sort of solution to the shortages. However, he had been raised with the understanding that the main work of a Tsar was to preserve the monarchy for his son. Thus, he decided on the very inopportune moment of late February, 1917 to try to disband the Duma and regain absolute power. When the Duma refused to disband, the High Commander of the army appealed to Nicholas, suggesting that he should abdicate before a full scale revolution broke out. Some suggested that the Tsar's cousin, Grand Duke Michael Alexandrovich would make an excellent replacement. He refused, however, and on March 1, Nicholas was forced to leave and was replaced with a Provisional Government which originally consisted of a mishmash of parliamentary figures and members of revolutionary councils that had been elected by workers, soldiers and peasants.

Lenin was still in exile in Zurich when the February Revolution pushed Nicholas II out of power, and he only found out about it on March 15. Understandably thrilled with this turn of events, Lenin began firing off missives to friends and allies in an attempt to harness the revolutionary energy and direct it toward an international class conflict, writing in one letter, "Spread out! Rouse new sections! Awaken fresh initiative, form new organisations in every stratum and prove to them that peace can come only with the armed Soviet of Workers' Deputies in power." At the same time, he and other members of the Provisional Government went about trying to secure his safe passage back to Russia, and eventually a Swiss colleague with contacts in the German Foreign Ministry was able to get Lenin a train ride into Russia. While that seems odd at first glance, it is apparent the German Foreign Ministry hoped that Lenin's agitation back in Russia would sufficiently distract the Russian Army and lead to their surrender to Germany or their quitting of the war.

The locomotive that brought Lenin back to Russia

Joining Lenin on his private train were 27 fellow Bolsheviks anxious to press forward the cause of socialism and shape the new political system. Passing through Germany, some passengers on the train were "struck by the total absence of grown-up men. Only women, teenagers and children could be seen at the wayside stations, on the fields, and in the streets of the towns." Lenin, however, was all about business. While on the train, he completed work on what became known as his famous April Theses, and he read them aloud as soon as he entered Petrograd on April 3rd. In it he outlined his plans for the immediate future:

1.In view of the undoubted honesty of the mass of rank and file representatives of revolutionary defencism who accept the war only as a necessity and not as a means of conquest, in view of their being deceived by the bourgeoisie, it is necessary most thoroughly, persistently, patiently to explain to them their error, to explain the inseparable connection between capital and the imperialist war, to prove that without the overthrow of capital it is impossible to conclude the war with a really democratic, non-oppressive peace.

2.The peculiarity of the present situation in Russia is that it represents a transition from the first stage of the revolution - which, because of the inadequate organization and insufficient class-consciousness of the proletariat, led to the assumption of power by the bourgeoisie - to its second stage which is to place power in the hands of the proletariat and the poorest strata of the peasantry.

3.No support to the Provisional Government; exposure of the utter falsity of all its promises, particularly those relating to the renunciation of annexations. Unmasking, instead of admitting, the illusion-breeding "demand" that this government, a

93

government of capitalist, should cease to be imperialistic.

4.Recognition of the fact that in most of the Soviets of Workers' Deputies our party constitutes a minority, and a small one at that, in the face of the bloc of all the petty bourgeois opportunist elements who have yielded to the influence of the bourgeoisie.

It must be explained to the masses that the Soviet of Workers' Deputies is the only possible form of revolutionary government and that, therefore, our task is, while this government is submitting to the influence of the bourgeoisie, to present a patient, systematic, and persistent analysis of its errors and tactics, an analysis especially adapted to the practical needs of the masses.

5.Not a parliamentary republic - a return to it from the Soviet of Workers' Deputies would be a step backward - but a republic of Soviets of Workers', Agricultural Labourers' and Peasants' Deputies throughout the land, from top to bottom.

Abolition of the police, the army, the bureaucracy. All officers to be elected and to be subject to recall at any time, their salaries not to exceed the average wage of a competent worker.

6.In the agrarian program, the emphasis must be shifted to the Soviets of Agricultural Laborers' Deputies [including]

a.Confiscation of private lands.

b.Nationalization of all lands in the country, and management of such lands by local Soviets of Agricultural Labourers' and Peasants' Deputies.

c.A separate organization of Soviets of Deputies of the poorest peasants.

d.Creation of model agricultural establishments out of large estates.

7.Immediate merger of all the banks in the country into one general national bank, over which the Soviet of Workers' Deputies should have control.

8.Not the "introduction" of Socialism as an immediate task, but the immediate placing of the Soviet of Workers' Deputies in control of social production and distribution of goods.

9.Party tasks [include] Immediate calling of a party convention and Changing the party program, mainly:

a.Concerning imperialism and the imperialist war.

b.Concerning our attitude toward the state, and our demand for a 'commune state."

c.Amending our antiquated minimum program.

10.Rebuilding the International. Taking the initiative in the creation of a revolutionary International, an International against the social-chauvinists and against the "center".

Although the turmoil had been limited to Russia so far, and the Theses were written about how to immediately create a socialist state in Russia, it's clear that Lenin envisioned an international revolution even at this early date. As one historian characterized his thinking in 1917, "Lenin made his revolution for the sake of Europe, not for the sake of Russia, and he expected Russia's preliminary revolution to be eclipsed when the international revolution took place. Lenin did not invent the iron curtain."

Lenin's April Theses were among the most radical writings of his life to date, and both Mensheviks and fellow Bolsheviks were taken aback. The Theses were roundly condemned by the Mensheviks (one of whom described them as the "ravings of a madman"), and initially the Theses were supported by only one prominent Bolshevik, Alexandra Kollontai.

Kollontai

One of the people that were concerned about Lenin's insistence on an immediate revolution was Joseph Stalin. While he had always been fascinated by Lenin's ideals, he was usually too pragmatic to begin a venture without an assurance of success. Stalin had been in exile himself until returning to Siberia, and by April 1917 he was the editor of the popular Bolshevik paper Pravda. Stalin could not remain silent forever. Though Stalin and other Bolsheviks still believed that the revolution should be a bourgeoise revolution, the Theses at least presented a party platform and a banner under which revolutionaries could rally and united. Thus, after wrestling with the issue for ten days, Stalin wrote a scathing article supporting Lenin and urging the peasants to rise up immediately. He further instructed them to begin by forming local committees that would confiscate large, privately owned estates and turn them over to the peasants that worked on them. Even still, Lenin was going in an ideologically different direction, one that brought him closer to the political leanings of Leon Trotsky.

Stalin

Trotsky's journey from New York to Russia was slowed by a last-ditch effort to keep him out of Russia by detaining him in Nova Scotia, but he arrived in May 1917. In the months that followed, he developed a closer relationships with the Bolsheviks, who at the time were a relatively weak and marginal player in the chaotic political scene. Soon after, he was arrested under orders from Kerensky, who distrusted him because of his fiery leadership of the Soviet and clear involvement in Bolshevik plots to seize power. However, Trotsky was not held long, and when he was released, his ferocious criticism of the Provisional Government was successful in swaying the urban workers and soldiers toward the Bolshevik position. He was about to become indispensable to Lenin.

Trotsky
The chaos continued when Alexander Kerensky, the new head of the Provisional Government, launched yet another military offensive against the Germans in July of 1917. Soldiers deserted by the thousands, with many of them carrying their government issued weapons back to the estates where they lived. They often used these guns to threaten or even kill their landlords so that they could have their land. They also burned stately mansions and moved ancient

boundary stones to create new, smaller farms for the peasants themselves to own.

Kerensky

Alarmed by the rioting and believing that it was a result of the impact Lenin and other revolutionaries were having on the common people, Kerensky outlawed the Bolsheviks and tried to round up its members, outlandishly accusing them of being German agents. Trotsky famously defended Lenin and other Bolsheviks against the charge, exhorting, "An intolerable atmosphere has been created, in which you, as well as we, are choking. They are throwing dirty accusations at Lenin and [Grigory] Zinoviev. Lenin has fought thirty years for the revolution. I have fought [for] twenty years against the oppression of the people. And we cannot but cherish a hatred for German militarism . . . I have been sentenced by a German court to eight months' imprisonment for my struggle against German militarism. This everybody knows. Let nobody in this hall say that we are hirelings of Germany." Luckily for Lenin, he got wind of the threat well enough ahead of time to escape to Finland, where he completed work on State and Revolution, an outline of the government he hoped to one day see in Russia.

Chapter 10: Lenin In Disguise In Finland, 1917
As the rioting was going on back at home, Kerensky's July Offensive failed miserably, and he came into conflict with his new general, Lavr Kornilov, over policies related to discipline and production. When Kornilov sent the troops under his command to march on Kerensky's headquarters in Petrograd, Kerensky had to appeal to the Bolsheviks for Red Guards to protect his capitol city. Lenin reluctantly agreed and immediately recruited more than 25,000 soldiers to protect the government he so vehemently opposed. When Kornilov's troops saw the rows of dug in Red Guards, they refused to advance, and Kornilov surrendered to the palace police.

Realizing that he now had the Provisional Government largely at his mercy, Lenin returned to Russia in October and set up a party headquarters in Smolny Institute for Girls in St. Petersburg. From there, he quietly ordered that the Provisional Government be deposed and the Winter Palace vacated. On the evening of October 25, the Second All-Russian Congress of Soviets met at the Smolny Institute to establish a new government. While there were initially some disagreements over the overthrow of the Provisional Government, Martov's Mensheviks and Lenin's Bolsheviks eventually agreed to share power. Ironically, after all the drama that had surrounded the earlier months of that year, the October Revolution went largely unnoticed. As Lenin had written a month earlier, "The peaceful development of any revolution is, generally speaking, extremely rare and difficult ... but ... a peaceful development of the revolution is possible and probable if all power is transferred to the Soviets. The struggle of parties for power within the Soviets may proceed peacefully, if the Soviets are made fully democratic." It seemed that way in October.

Lenin arrived at the meeting the next evening to thunderous applause, appearing without a disguise for the first time since July. Famous American journalist John Reed, who would later chronicle the Russian Revolution in his critically acclaimed book, Ten Days That Shook The World, described Lenin for readers. "A short, stocky figure, with a big head set down in his shoulders, bald and bulging. Little eyes, a snubbish nose, wide, generous mouth, and heavy chin; clean-shaven now, but already beginning to bristle with the well-known beard of his past and future. Dressed in shabby clothes, his trousers much too long for him. Unimpressive, to be the idol of a mob, loved and revered as perhaps few leaders in history have been. A strange popular leader—a leader purely by virtue of intellect; colourless, humourless, uncompromising and detached, without picturesque idiosyncrasies—but with the power of explaining profound ideas in simple terms, of analysing a concrete situation. And combined with shrewdness, the greatest intellectual audacity."

Beginning his speech with "We shall now proceed to construct the Socialist order!", at the meeting, Lenin proposed a "Decree on Peace" calling for an end of the war, and a "Decree on Land" announcing that all property owned by large land owners and the aristocracy would be given to the peasants. Both decrees passed with little dissension. Next, the new government elected a Bolshevik majority to the Council of People's Commissars, with the Mensheviks joining the government a few weeks later. Lenin was soon elected Chairman of the Council, making him head of the government, though he had originally intended for the position to go to Trotsky, who declined because he worried his Jewish ethnicity would pose problems.

In recognition of his contribution, the now totally empowered Lenin appointed Stalin the Commissar of Nationalities, joking with him about his meteoric rise to power. As Commissar, Stalin was in charge of all the non-Russian people in the country, including Buriats, Byelorussians, Georgians, Tadzhiks, Ukrainians and Yakuts, nearly half the country's population. The spoiled little boy who'd been forced to speak Russian and had been teased about his appearance was now a bitter, angry man with nearly unlimited power. The combination would not make for a pretty outcome.

Initially, however, it looked like all would be well for these foreigners under Russian control. He concluded his famous Helsinki address of 1917 with these words of encouragement and promises of support:

"Comrades! Information has reached us that your country is experiencing approximately the same crisis of power as Russia experienced on the eve of the October Revolution. Information has reached us that attempts are being made to frighten you too

105

with the bogey of famine, sabotage, and so on. Permit me to tell you on the basis of the practical experience of the revolutionary movement in Russia that these dangers, even if real, are by no means insuperable! These dangers can be overcome if you act resolutely and without faltering. In the midst of war and economic disruption, in the midst of the revolutionary movement which is flaring up in the West and of the increasing victories of the workers' revolution in Russia, there are no dangers or difficulties that could withstand your onslaught. In such a situation only one power, socialist power, can maintain itself and conquer. In such a situation only one kind of tactics can be effective, the tactics of Danton—audacity, audacity and again audacity! And if you should need our help, you will have it—we shall extend you a fraternal hand. Of this you may rest assured."

Unfortunately, the non-Russian peoples who heard or read this speech remained unconvinced. They were not so much interested in Russian help as they were national determination. Therefore they proved to be a constant source of stress to the new Commissar, setting up their own governments, opposing Bolshevik policy, and overall acting with the self-determination they had been promised, as long as they determined to join the new Union of Soviet Socialist Republics.

Faced with this level of opposition to his and the other Bolsheviks' plans, Stalin took a different tact. Accusing the new independent governments of being under the control of "the bourgeoisie," he agreed with Lenin that a more centralized government was needed.

As the Russian Civil War played out during the early 1920s, Stalin became more involved in military matters while Lenin continued to focus on politics.

Trotsky, meanwhile, had become chairman of the Petrograd Soviet in St. Petersburg (which had its name changed to Petrograd during World War I to sound less German). Trotsky regained his reputation as a fiery and charismatic speaker with great sway over the city's working class. At the same time, during and after his prison stint, he solidified his relations with the Bolsheviks and Lenin and finally joined the party, ending his status as a factionless coalition-builder and severing his earlier ties to the Mensheviks, who had been allied with Kerensky's governing coalition.

Ironically, Lenin did not think there would be be a need to create a political police force or external intelligence agency. In this, he was joined by Trotsky, who initially ordered the publication of the secret treaties signed by the tsarist government and asserted that "the rejection of secret diplomacy is the main condition for an honest, popular, genuinely democratic foreign policy" (Simbirdzev, 2017). Lenin's pre-revolutionary idea of life in Bolshevik Russia was nothing more than a utopia. In The State and Revolution, written in the summer of 1917, he had argued that in the future there will be no place for the police, especially for the secret police. But things drastically changed when the Bolshevik leaders collided with reality. The fundamental element of the Soviet state was the communist myth that, as the vanguard of the proletariat, the Bolsheviks led a popular uprising that expressed the will not only of the Bolsheviks themselves, but of the entire Russian people. Actually, the October Revolution was nothing more than a coup d'état, committed by a revolutionary minority overthrowing the Provisional Government which itself had replaced the tsarist regime.

Neither Lenin nor his followers could accept this reality. Overthrowing the government that had lost the confidence of the people, the Bolsheviks still could not get or maintain the support of the vast majority. In the Constituent Assembly elections held immediately after the revolution, their main left opponents were the Socialist-Revolutionaries, who achieved the absolute majority of votes, while the Bolsheviks were able to win the support of less than a quarter of voters. Even in alliance with the Socialist-Revolutionaries, they remained in the minority, so they dissolved the Constituent Assembly, convened in January 1918.

Having seen how easily a multi-generational dynasty fell, Lenin was obviously concerned about keeping his own infant administration safe. Lenin did not expect that the new Bolshevik government (the Council of People's Commissars) would face such internal and external opposition, which is ultimately what led to his decition to create a "special machine" for solving this problem. Convinced of the uniqueness and exceptional correctness of Marxist doctrine, the Bolshevik leaders viewed any opposition, regardless of its social roots, as a threat of counter-revolution.

On December 19, it became known that a general strike of civil servants was coming. This news made the Council of People's Commissars and its chairman Lenin take more radical measures. Felix Dzerzhinsky received the instruction to create a special commission to resolve such kind of problems and combat counter-revolution. The next day, December 20, Lenin wrote to Dzerzhinsky, "The bourgeoisie intends to commit the most heinous crime..." Addressing the Council of People's Commissars on the same day, Dzerzhinsky required the creation of the commission to combat counter-revolution: "Do not think that I'm looking for forms of revolutionary justice. We do not need justice now, there is a war on the face to face, a war to the end, life or death (Archive of the Cheka, 2007).

Dzerzhinsky

Yakov Peters, Józef Unszlicht, Abram Belenky (standing), Dzerzhinsky, and Vyacheslav Menzhinsky at the presidium of the Cheka in 1921

Thus, the Council of People's Commissars approved the creation, under the leadership of Dzerzhinsky, of the All-Russian Extraordinary Commission for Combating Counter-Revolution and Sabotage, known subsequently as the Extraordinary Commission. Known colloquially as the Cheka (Extraordinary Commission), it soon became as feared by non-socialists as the Tsar's secret police had ever been. In addition to monitoring the movements of anyone opposing the government, the Cheka also enforced censorship laws against non-socialist newspapers.

The KGB has created a kind of cult of personality out of Dzerzhinskiy. In his address was uttered more words of praise than to all his followers taken together. Calling him the "knight of the revolution, Soviet historian V. Andrianov wrote, "There are many people who deserve this title, but despite this, every time we uttered these words, we primarily think of F. Dzerzhinsky ... Throughout his heroic life, he paved the way to immortality" (Sever, 2008).

Like most of the early leaders of the Cheka, Dzerzhinsky was not Russian by nationality. He was born in 1877 in the family of Polish intellectuals-landowners. In his early childhood, he believed that his vocation was to become a Catholic priest. However at school he became interested in Marxism and in 1895 joined the ranks of the Lithuanian Social-Democratic Party. In 1900 he became one of the founders of the Social Democratic Party of Poland and Lithuania (SDPiL), led by the famous German-Polish Marxist theorist Rosa Luxemburg. This party advocated not for the independence of Poland, but for proletarian internationalism and cooperation with Russian Marxists. He joined the Bolsheviks, first as a delegate to the SDPiL, and then he was elected to the Central Committee of the Bolshevik Party at the summer party conference of 1917. Later, Dzerzhinsky took an active part in the October Revolution.

Luxemburg
During his first year as head of the Cheka, Dzerzhinsky was working and living in his office in the Lubyanka in Moscow, and thanks to his Spartan lifestyle, he received the nickname "Iron Felix". The old Chekist (member of Cheka) Fyodor Timofeevich Fomin later reported with admiration that Dzerzhinsky refused to enjoy the privileges that the other Chekists did not have (Gordievskiy & Andru, 1992). Like Lenin, Dzerzhinsky was extremely efficient, and willing to sacrifice himself and others in the

name of the ideals of the revolution. Viktor Chebrikov, chairman of the KGB from 1982-1988, stated, "Felix Edmundovich wanted to eradicate injustice and crimes on earth and dreamed of those times when wars and national enmity would disappear forever from our lives." (Ibid).

The cult of Dzerzhinsky was created immediately after his death in 1926. The portrait of Dzerzhinsky and his military uniform were placed in a glass coffin and exhibited in the conference room of the KGB officer club as an object of worship. During the celebration of the 20th anniversary of the Cheka in December 1937, Dzerzhinsky was called "an indefatigable Bolshevik, an inflexible knight of the revolution, under whose leadership the Cheka repeatedly seized the mortal threat hanging over the young Soviet Republic." (Archive of the Cheka, 2007).

The cult of Stalin gradually supplanted the image of Dzerzhinsky. Soon after World War II, his portrait and posthumous mask were removed from the KGB officer's club, but the policy of de-Stalinization during the 1960s marked the beginning of the revival of the cult of Dzerzhinsky. The KGB tried in every possible way to dissociate itself from the bloody role that he played in the immediate wake of Lenin's death as Stalin took control, and a mythical portrait was created, depicting Dzerzhinsky (Saint Felix), as a "knight of the revolution" killing the dragon of the counter-revolution.

Dzerzhinsky's words that the Chekist should have a "hot heart, a cold head and clean hands" were transferred from one monument to another (Gordievskiy & Andru, 1992). In the late 1950s, opposite the central building of the KGB in Dzerzhinsky Square, a large statue of Dzerzhinsky was erected.

The main means approved by the Council of People's Commissars on December 20, 1917, which the Cheka had to use to fight the counter-revolution, were "seizure of property, resettlement, deprivation of cards, publication of lists of enemies of the people, etc". Nevertheless, the main weapon of the Cheka was terror. Lenin did not imagine the scale of the opposition he would have to face after the revolution, and he quickly came to the conclusion that "a special system of organized violence" must be created to implement the dictatorship of the proletariat.

Lenin brutally criticized the "prejudices on the death penalty." (Ibid)

All the while, Lenin believed that the masses had healthier instincts. In December 1917, Lenin suggested that the masses should execute their own court ("street court") over "speculators". He strongly encouraged all actions, including terror, directed against "class enemies". One of his closest associates, Martin Yanovich Latsis, wrote in the newspaper Krasny Terror, "We do not wage war against individual people, we are destroying the bourgeoisie as a class. (Ibid)

In January 1918, despite objections from Lenin and Dzerzhinsky, the representatives of the Left Socialist-Revolutionaries in the Council of People's Commissars insisted on their party representation in the Cheka. One of the four left-wing Socialist-Revolutionaries appointed by members of the Cheka board, Vyacheslav Alekseevich Alexandrovich, became the deputy of Dzerzhinsky. In March 1918, after signing peace with Germany in Brest-Litovsk, as a sign of protest, the Left Socialist-Revolutionaries withdrew from the Council of People's Commissars. The Bolshevik Party changed its name to the Communist Party. Since then, the Council of

People's Commissars was composed exclusively of Communists, and the Bolshevik government moved the capital from Petrograd to Moscow, ironically in part because its treaty with Germany ending the war placed potential enemy forces too close to Petrograd for comfort.

Despite the fact that the Left Socialist Revolutionaries left the government, they were still a part of the Cheka, and Dzerzhinsky fully trusted his deputy, Aleksandrovich. After moving to Moscow, he handed over to him the full power of solving daily administrative issues, and he concentrated on his operational work.

One of the first victims of the Chekist terror in Moscow was the famous circus clown Bim-Bom, who often laughed at the Communists. As it would be with the KGB, the Cheka did not understand such humor and considered it as an ideological provocation. When the Chekists with stony faces approached Bim-Bom, viewers thought that this was only part of the overall performance, but their laughter soon gave way to a panic when they heard the shots. The Chekists opened fire on Bim-Bohm, who was trying to escape.

In addition to terror, in the fight against counter-revolution, the Cheka often used the agents. Although Dzerzhinsky opposed the royal (tsarist) methods of using agent provocateurs, he very quickly became a real expert in this field. According to KGB sources, the first significant success of the Cheka using its agents was an operation against an organization that was in Petrograd known as the "Union to Combat the Bolsheviks".

A Chekist known as Golubev, posing as a former officer of the tsarist army, was able to quickly penetrate into the Union, expose many of its members, and reveal the places of their secret encounters. During January and February, the entire "Union", numbering about 4,000 people, was exposed by the Chekists and completely neutralized with the help of the Red Guards. The Bolsheviks believed that the entire Western capitalist world was revolting against them with all its might, and the Chekists believed they would play the decisive role in protecting the young Soviet state in its struggle against the gigantic conspiracies of the Western capital system and its secret services.

In spite of the Cheka's best efforts, those who opposed Lenin and the Bolsheviks were still out there, and they were gunning for Lenin, literally. In January 1918, gunmen shot at Lenin and Fritz Platten as they sat in an automobile after Lenin had given a speech, which Lenin survived after Platten pushed him down and shielded him. But the most famous assassination attempt would come in August 1918, when a supporter of the Socialist Revolutionary Party, Fanya Kaplan, approached Lenin as he sat in an automobile. After calling to him to get his attention, she fired at him three times, hitting him once in the arm and once in the jaw and neck. Though the wounds rendered him unconscious, Lenin survived the shooting, and fearful of people at the hospital who might try to finish the job, he returned to the Kremilin and ordered physicians to come there to treat him where he felt safe. Ultimately, doctors refused to perform surgery given the precarious position of the bullet in his neck. Pravda used the attempt for propaganda purposes, reporting, "Lenin, shot through twice, with pierced lungs spilling blood, refuses help and goes on his own. The next morning, still threatened with death, he reads papers, listens, learns, and observes to see that the engine of the locomotive that carries us towards global revolution has not stopped working..."

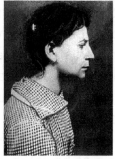

Fanya Kaplan

Despite that, Soviet officials began to downplay the attack, and many across Russia never learned of it. Though he survived the attack, the bullets were left in place and continued to erode his health. However, Lenin kept working and appearing in public, determined to keep the public ignorant of how weak his condition was becoming. This was important because Lenin was increasingly viewed as the embodiment of the new regime, and it was feared that his death could cause everything to crumble. One former Tsarist wrote as much, reporting after the attempt, "As it happens, the attempt to kill Lenin has made him much more popular than he was. One hears a great many people, who are far from having any sympathy with the Bolsheviks, saying that it would be an absolute disaster if Lenin had succumbed to his wounds, as it was first thought he would. And they are quite right, for, in the midst of all this chaos and confusion, he is the backbone of the new body politic, the main support on which everything rests.."

The Bolsheviks may have downplayed the assassination attempt publicly, but they were privately plotting retaliation on a massive scale. Two weeks before Kaplan's attempt on Lenin's life, the Petrograd Cheka chief Moisei Uritsky had been assassinated, and now Stalin suggested to Lenin that they should engage in "open and systematic mass terror…[against] those responsible." Thus, the Cheka, under the instruction of Stalin, launched what later came to be known as the "Red Terror" in response to the assassination attempt. In the weeks that followed, more than 800 people were executed, including the entire Romanov family. This however, was just the beginning.

As the Bolsheviks, known popularly as the Red Russians fought an ongoing war against those who opposed socialism (the White Russians), more than 18,000 people were executed on charges related to opposing Lenin and his rule. While historians have often debated the extent of Lenin's personal involvement in the executions, Trotsky himself later asserted that it was Lenin who authorized the execution of the Russian Royal Family.

Though he is often remembered as a vocal opponent of Stalin's terror (and ultimately a victim of it), Trotsky was fully in support of the Cheka's methods and even took time to write and publish a full-throated defense of them in the book Terrorism and Communism (1920). He also defended the policies of "War Communism," including large-scale confiscation of produce, livestock, and grains in order to fuel the war effort, practices that placed a devastating burden on the rural poor in particular. Trotsky summed up his defense of all of these measures in Terrorism and Communism: "The more perfect the revolution, the greater are the masses it draws in; and the longer it is prolonged, the greater is the destruction it achieves in the apparatus of production, and the more terrible inroads does it make upon public resources. From this there follows merely the conclusion which did not require proof – that a civil war is harmful to economic life.

Chapter 11: Victims Of The Red Terror

Imperial Germany was the only power that established official diplomatic relations with the Bolshevik regime and exchanged ambassadors after the signing of the peace the treaty in Brest-Litovsk. On April 23, 1918 in Moscow, the German Embassy was opened, headed by Graph Wilhelm Mirbach.

The task of penetrating the German embassy was entrusted to the counter-intelligence department, created in May 1918 in the framework of combating counter-revolution. In 1921-1922 the counterintelligence department (abbreviated as KRO) was expanded and become the predecessor of the Second Main Directorate of the KGB. At the head of this department was the twenty-year-old left-wing Socialist-Revolutionary Yakov Blumkin, perhaps the youngest head of the department in the history of the KGB. Blumkin successfully carried out the operation to penetrate the German embassy, having come into contact with Count Robert Mirbach, an Austrian relative of the German ambassador, who was captured during the war. In June, Blumkin received from him a written commitment to supply the Cheka with secret information about Germany and the activities of the German embassy.

However, Dzerzhinsky acted unreasonably, entrusting this operation to Blumkin, since the Left Socialist-Revolutionaries continued to actively oppose the Brest-Litovsk Peace Agreement. On July 4, the Central Committee of the Left SRs approved the plan of the assassination of the German ambassador. The Left SRs believed that by killing him they would force the Bolsheviks to stop the "pacification" of the Germans and resume military operations on the Eastern Front, which, in their opinion, would contribute to the cause of the development of the world revolution.

The attempt was directed to Blumkin and his collaborator, photographer, left-wing Socialist-Revolutionary, Nikolai Andreev. On the morning of July 6, Blumkin prepared a document on the letterhead of the Cheka, with the forged signature of Dzerzhinsky and the secretary of the Cheka, instructing him and Andreev to negotiate with the German ambassador.

Dzerzhinsky's assistant, the Left Socialist-Revolutionary Aleksandrovich, who was involved in this conspiracy by Bliumkin, put an official seal of the Cheka on this document. In the afternoon of the same day Blyumkin and Andreev came to the German embassy and agreed to meet with the ambassador under the pretext of having to discuss the matter connected with his relative Count Robert Mirbach. Later Blumkin claimed that he killed the ambassador from his revolver, however, according to the embassy's staff, all three shots done by Blumkin failed to achieve the goal, and Count Wilhelm Mirbach was killed by Andreev. (Sever, 2008).

Thus, instead of defending a new communist state, in July 1918 the Cheka almost did not play the role of an instrument for its destruction. In a telegram to Stalin, Lenin wrote that the assassination of Mirbach put Russia on "the verge of a resumption of war with Germany" (Archive of the Cheka, 2007). The assassination was followed by the uprising of the Left Socialist-Revolutionaries, as a result of which the building of the Cheka in the Lubyanka was seized, and Dzerzhinsky was arrested. But the Left SRs had no clear plan of action, and their rebellion was suppressed within 24 hours by Communists Latvian troops.

On July 8, at his own request, Dzerzhinsky resigned from his post as head of the Cheka. A commission was set up to investigate the circumstances of the uprising, and the Cheka was cleaned of the Left SRs. August 22 Dzerzhinsky was again appointed to the post of chairman of the Cheka. By this time, the Cheka consisted exclusively of Communists. The restraining influence of the Left Socialist-Revolutionaries had lost its force, and the policy of terror against political enemies had been developed.

Meanwhile, the forces of the so-called White Army, made up of anti-Bolshevik Russians of all stripes and their allies from nearly all the major European nations, combined to place the new revolutionary regime in a state of siege. In response, the Bolsheviks introduced a number of policies that would set the stage for the state terrorism and suppression of later years.

White Army propaganda poster depicting Trotsky as Satan

Unfortunately, bullets weren't all that was killing the Russian common people. While the Whites and Reds engaged in a civil war that would last for nearly 7 years, ordinary Russians were starving due to war time communism measures that allowed the Soviet government to confiscate food for soldiers from peasant farms with little or no payment. When the farmers retaliated by growing fewer crops, the Cheka responded by executing or imprisoning the offending peasants. However, even the Cheka could not cause plants to grow, and during the Famine of 1921, more than 5 million Russians starved to death in and near their own homes. This tragedy, along with the civil unrest it provoked, led Lenin to institute the New

Economic Policy to rejuvenate the both agriculture and industry.

As this all suggests, the cruelty of the Cheka can be compared with Stalin's NKVD (People's Commissariat of Internal Affairs of the USSR), although the scale of the massacres was much less at this time. While Dzerzhinsky and his assistants resorted to the Red Terror only as an objectively necessary means of class struggle, some of the ordinary members of the Cheka, especially in the provinces, enjoyed the power of cruelty without going into high ideological discourse. Yakov Khristoforovich Peter, one of Dzerzhinsky's first and most prominent assistants, later recognized the existence of "many dishonest elements" in the Cheka (Archive of the Cheka, 2007).

Reorganizing the Cheka

The Cheka's badge in the early 1920s
By the beginning of the 1920s, the White Guard forces no longer posed a serious threat to the Bolshevik regime, although they were not completely destroyed. The decree signed by Lenin and Dzerzhinsky abolished the death penalty for "enemies of Soviet power," but three weeks later Lenin changed his mind. At a meeting of representatives of the local Cheka, he said that the death penalty was only "a necessary measure", which, most likely, would also be needed for further struggle against "counter-revolutionary movements." (Archive of the Cheka, 2007). In the official history of the KGB, it says, "Thanks to the determined struggle of the Cheka authorities, the plans of the White Poles were failed, aimed at undermining the Red Army's fighting efficiency through espionage, sabotage and banditry." (Ibid)

Between 1917 and 1921, more than 250,000 people became victims of the Cheka, but by 1921, when the victory of the Bolsheviks in the Civil War was no longer in doubt, many members of the party believed that the Cheka's time had passed. Naturally, the Chekists opposed the thought of disbanding, and although the growth of the Cheka was temporarily stopped, and its rights were limited, it still managed to survive, albeit in a slightly modified form. The 9th All-Russian Congress of Soviets noted on December 28, 1921 that "the strengthening of Soviet power in the country and abroad has made it possible to reduce the functions of the Cheka and its bodies." (Ibid).

Soviet Russia began to take a number of steps to implement a large-scale program of secret activities outside the country even before systematic collection of information on the channels of foreign intelligence was established. While the Cheka was protecting the Bolshevik regime from real and imaginary enemies within the country, the activities of Soviet agents abroad were primarily aimed at spreading the revolution. At the same time, most foreign secret operations were organized not by the Cheka, but by the Comintern, the Communist International, which was under the control of the Bolsheviks. The Executive Committee of the Comintern (IKKI) called itself the "General Staff of the World Revolution." (Collins, 1998). The collection of intelligence information abroad had become increasingly important. Despite the considerable successes of Soviet espionage activity in the 1920s, the main object of the Cheka's activity from the first day of its foundation was "counterrevolution", and not capitalist governments. Until the end of the Civil War, the main threat of counterrevolution came from within Russia itself, but with the evacuation of the last White Guard armies in November 1920, the counter-revolutionary centers moved abroad. On December 1, 1920, Lenin instructed Dzerzhinsky to develop a plan for the neutralization of these centers. Four days later, Dzerzhinsky presented a multi-purpose plan of action. He offered to take more hostages from family members of eminent Russian emigres, create special detachments to attack its leaders, and expand operations with the use of agent-provocateurs.

Thus, on December 20, 1920, the third anniversary of the Cheka's establishment, Dzerzhinsky decided to create the Foreign Department (better known as INO). On February 8, 1922, the Cheka was transformed into the State Political Administration (GPU), which became part of the People's Commissariat of Internal Affairs (NKVD). Dzerzhinsky, who headed the Commissariat of

Internal Affairs and the Cheka since March 1919, became the head of the GPU.

Officially, the rights of the GPU were significantly reduced in comparison with what the Cheka had. The field of activity of the GPU was narrowed to the organization and conduct of subversive operations, while all issues related to criminal offenses were now settled by courts and revolutionary tribunals. The GPU was given the right only to conduct an investigation, meaning it was no longer able to pass sentence without trial or exile people to concentration camps administratively.

Ultimately, however, the GPU was gradually able to regain most of the rights that the Cheka had, and this was done with the blessing of Lenin. After the creation of the USSR in 1923, the GPU was given the status of a union body (United State Political Administration, abbreviated OGPU). Unlike the Cheka, conceived as a temporarily necessary means to protect the revolution in its infancy, the GPU, OGPU and their followers occupied one of the central places in the Soviet state system.

Stalin and Spying

In 1926, Dzerzhinsky died of a heart attack, and Vyacheslav Rudolfovich Menzhinsky was appointed in place of Dzerzhinsky. At first glance, both Dzerzhinsky and Menzhinsky had much in common, most notably as old Bolsheviks and descendants of wealthy Polish families. Menzhinsky became a member of the Cheka board shortly after its foundation and was appointed as the first deputy of Dzerzhinsky when he became chairman of the OGPU. He may also have been the most educated among the leaders of the KGB - Menzhinsky was fluent in 12 languages when he was hired by the Cheka, and he subsequently learned Chinese, Japanese, Persian and Turkish. He was also interested in physics, chemistry, astronomy, and mathematics.

Menzhinsky

Menzhinsky was not a follower of Stalin's, which would naturally put him in a precarious position moving forward. During the Civil War, he met Trotsky at the front and warned that Stalin was leading a "very complicated game" against him. However, he never seriously opposed the growing power of Stalin.

Before his new appointment, Menzhinsky was suffering from asthma, so he often met visitors while lying on the couch in his office in Lubyanka. In April 1929, Menzhinsky suffered a heart attack that sidelined him for two years. In 1931, he returned to perform his duties, but his health did not allow him to

work hard.

Due to Menzhinsky's poor health and his sluggish leadership, the power in the OGPU gradually shifted to his more aggressive deputy, Henry Grigorevich Yagoda. According to Aghabekov, if Menzhinsky had no equal in breadth of education, Yagoda had no equal in cruelty, lack of culture, and rudeness (Ibid). However, these traits had not yet manifested themselves so clearly when Dzerzhinsky appointed him as his second deputy in 1923. Perhaps Dzerzhinsky believed that he was simply an executive and energetic bureaucrat, full of ambition, but if so, Yagoda became a classic example of a bureaucrat spoiled by

excessive power.

Yagoda

Stalin never completely trusted Yagoda and bided his time waiting for a convenient moment to change the head of the OGPU. Stalin was able to negotiate with Yagoda, who was more a careerist than an ideologist and was ready to follow Stalin merely to climb the social ladder. At the same time, he was not ready to support Stalin unconditionally.

During its first year under the leadership of Menzhinsky and Yagoda, the OGPU successfully completed an operation called "Trust," but this success was overshadowed by a number of scandalous exposures and failures of Soviet foreign intelligence. In the spring of 1927, a sensational exposure of Soviet agents took place in 8 different countries. That March, an espionage organization was uncovered in Poland, led by a former White Army general who later became an agent of the OGPU named Daniel Vetrenko. Around the same time, the leading specialist of the Soviet-Turkish corporation in Istanbul was accused of organizing espionage on the Turkish-Iraqi border. Shortly after, the Swiss police announced the arrest of two Soviet spies, and in April, during a search conducted at the Soviet consulate in Beijing, a huge number of documents on Soviet espionage activities were found. The French "Surte" also arrested 8 members of the Soviet espionage network headed by Jean Creme, a member of the Politburo of the French

Communist Party. In May, officers of the Austrian Ministry of Foreign Affairs were detained, and they supplied the OGPU agents with secret information. And as a result of a raid and search conducted by British special services in London on the premises of the All-Russian Cooperative Society ("Arcos") and the Soviet trade delegation, William Joneson-Hicks, the Minister of Internal Affairs of the Great Britain, claimed that "one of the biggest and most nefarious espionage organizations was disclosed." (Gordievskiy & Andru, 1992).

The police raids in Beijing and London, followed by the publication of some intelligence information, dealt a strong blow to the Soviet foreign spy network. The documents published in China contained a lot of scandalous details about the activities of the Soviet secret agencies (mainly military intelligence), including instructions received from Moscow that "no measures, including robbery and massacres, should be avoided" in promoting conflict between the Chinese people and Western countries (Ibid). They also contained lists of agents' names, instructions to Chinese communists to assist in conducting intelligence operations, and detailed descriptions of weapons secretly imported into China.

The exposures of Soviet spies had another serious consequence, as relations between the Soviet Union and Great Britain were formally broken. The USSR used to consider Great Britain as the world's leading power, but the exposure of activities of the Soviet military intelligence in 1927 was the last straw. On May 26, 1927, Austen Chamberlain informed the Soviet attorney Arkady Rozengolts that the British government was breaking diplomatic relations with the Soviet Union, since it conducted "anti-British, espionage activities and propaganda." (Ibid).

The exposure of Soviet intelligence in the spring of 1927 had a significant impact on Stalin, who viewed it all as evidence of a deep imperialist conspiracy. He claimed, "There is no doubt that the main question of our time is the question of the threat of an imperialist war. This is not some kind of unreal, immaterial 'danger' of a new war. This is a very real, material threat of war in general and war against the Soviet Union in particular." According to Stalin, the first organizer of the "United Imperialist Front" against the Soviet Union was its main enemy, "the British bourgeoisie and its general headquarters—the Conservative Party." In response, the OGPU, as the "shield and sword of the revolution," would be called upon to disclose and expose the inevitable imperialist conspiracies and nip them in the bud.

For the first time, Stalin used the OGPU to strengthen his power within the Communist Party. Like the Cheka, the OGPU aimed to combat the counter-revolution, but now, the definition of the counter-revolution had changed. Under Lenin, the counter-revolution meant an opposition to the Communist Party, whereas under Stalin, it simply meant opposition to Stalin himself. Since many Communists were opposed to Stalin, the OGPU used the same methods of penetration and provocation inside the party that had previously been used against enemies of the party.

The first victims were members of the "Left Opposition," headed by Trotsky and Zinoviev. In November 1927, Trotsky, Zinoviev, and almost 100 of their followers were expelled from the party. Zinoviev agreed to repent and renounce "Trotskyism," after which he was reinstated in the ranks of the party. Trotsky refused to do so, and in January 1928, he was

139

exiled by the OGPU to a remote region of Kazakhstan along the border with China.

Zinoviev

Having finished with the "Left Opposition," Stalin aimed to realize his radical policy of the Socialist reorganization of the Soviet economy. Addressing the Central Committee in November 1928, Stalin insisted that the survival of Socialism in a country depended on the ability of the Soviet economy to overtake the West.

Meanwhile, a new threat of external aggression spurred the hunt of internal saboteurs who had entered into an alliance with foreigners, especially with the French "imperialists." On September 22, 1930, it was announced in the press that the OGPU had discovered a "counter-revolutionary society" consisting of 48 professors, agronomists, and heads of food enterprises, led by Professor Alexander Ryazantsev. All of them were accused of disrupting food supplies and were shot.

Stalin and many members of the OGPU continued to believe the counter-revolutionary conspiracies of traitors and foreign enemies were part of a long-term plan for sabotaging the Soviet economy. In March 1933, six English electrical engineers of the Metropolitan Vickers Company who had worked on the construction of one of Russia's industrial facilities were charged with sabotage and espionage and arrested as a result. In response, the British government announced a trade embargo, which was canceled in July 1933 after the British engineers were released.

In July 1934, the OGPU was renamed the GUGB (Main Directorate of State Security) and transferred to the newly opened NKVD (People's Commissariat of Internal Affairs) headed by Yagoda. Thus, the political police, the regular police, the criminal investigation service, the border troops, the internal troops, and the entire criminal system all became subordinate to one body in October 1934, and the NKVD became synonymous with the political police, although it was formally a part of the latter. This powerful machine was personally and directly subordinate to Stalin, who had a direct line of communication with the NKVD through his personal secretariat, headed by Alexander Poskrebyshev.

In 1936, Nikolai Ezhov replaced Yagoda as chairman of the NKVD and headed the "Great Terror." The murder of Sergey Kirov, Stalin's main potential opponent, led to an even greater strengthening of the NKVD's power. On December 1, 1934, Kirov was shot from behind as he left his office in the central building of the party organization in Leningrad. Leonid Nikolaev, his assassin, considered himself a follower of the "populists" who had committed the assassination of Tsar Alexander II and had obvious mental problems.

Kirov

Shortly before the assassination, Nikolaev was twice detained by Kirov's guards and released both times on orders from the Leningrad NKVD, despite the fact that a loaded revolver had been found in his briefcase. None of the KGB officers had any doubt that Stalin personally gave the order to kill Kirov, and many believe Stalin decided not to give this case to Yagoda, whom he did not fully trust. Instead, he acted through the head of the Leningrad NKVD, Philip Medved, and his deputy, I. Zaporozhets (Gordievskiy and Andru, 1992).

After Kirov's assassination, a directive came into force the same evening requiring the immediate punishment of all those suspected of terrorism, including the death penalty. According to Nikita Khrushchev, this directive came out "without the approval of the Politburo," meaning it was Stalin's personal initiative. Thus, the NKVD gained power over the life and death of Soviet citizens. For the next

20 years, the NKVD determined who was a "terrorist" and who was not.

The first victims of the NKVD, those accused of Kirov's death, were the so-called White Guard conspirators who had penetrated Russia through the border with Poland, Finland, and Latvia. 104 fictional conspirators were captured and shot.

In 1935, Stalin aimed to organize massive attacks on the existing and potential opposition to his regime. The purge of the party in 1933 and 1934 was mainly aimed at eradicating "corruption," and in 1935, the purge intensified and became more politicized. At Stalin's behest in the summer of 1936, the Central Committee approved a secret resolution giving the NKVD the extraordinary power to destroy all "enemies of the people."

Nikolai Ivanovich Yezhov who had come to replace Yagoda, was the first Russian to become the head of the KGB. As secretary of the Central Committee and head of the Control Commission, Yezhov had supervised the activities of the NKVD on behalf of Stalin. He also created a security service parallel to the NKVD inside the party apparatus.

During Yezhov's time, all restrictions preventing the elimination of Stalin's imaginary enemies were removed. On June 11, it was announced that Marshal Tukhachevsky, a hero of the Russian Civil War and a leading Soviet military strategist, was arrested, along with seven other generals, on charges of treason. They were apparently shot the next day, and Marshal Voroshilov reported that the traitors had "confessed to their crimes, sabotage and espionage."(Gordievskiy and Andru, 1992). As it was later announced, they'd conspired with Trotsky and Nazi Germany.

Yezhov

The most dangerous "enemies of the people" were the employees of three organizations called upon to defend the Soviet state, the party, the Red Army, and the NKVD. 110 of the 139 members of the Central Committee elected at the party Congress in 1934 were shot or sentenced to imprisonment. Perhaps not surprisingly, only 59 of 1,966 delegates took part in the work of the next Congress in 1939. 75 of the 80 members of the Revolutionary Military Council were shot, and more than half of the officers of the Red Army, probably more than 35,000 people, were shot or imprisoned. The top leadership of the NKVD itself was changed twice (ibid).

Under Yezhov, all 18 state security commissioners of the first and second ranks who had served under Yagoda were shot, with the exception of Slutsky, who was poisoned. Of the 122 top officers serving from 1937-1938, only 21 officers managed to maintain their position after Yezhov himself fell victim to Stalin's purges and was executed in 1940. During his leadership, anything that remained of the first Cheka leaders' idealism had been destroyed. Yezhov was convinced their cruelty was necessary for building a new society and fighting counter-revolution.

Victims of the NKVD were both Russian and foreign Communists. Most of the representatives of the Comintern and foreign communist parties in Moscow were exposed as "enemy agents" or "foreign spies" and shot. The most vulnerable were members of illegal Communist parties and their families, as they could not count on the support of the countries from which they had come. Most of them had been sentenced to prisons abroad and were therefore accused of being recruited by capitalist special services.

Of all the illegal parties, the most fictitious of spies were among the leadership of the Polish and Yugoslav Communist Parties. Polish Communists caused the greatest suspicion, as there were many Jews among their leaders who took Trotsky's side after Lenin's death, and they were shot. Stalin also did not trust the Yugoslav

Communist Party, headed by S. Markovich, who, in 1925, opposed the Stalinist approach to the solution of the national question. Paradoxically, Stalin used to trust Marshal Tito, the Communist leader in Yugoslavia.

Tito

The last large-scale exposure of a fictional international counter-revolutionary conspiracy against Stalin's Russia came in February 1938 with the trial of 21 members of the "bloc of Rightists and Trotskyists." The main defendants were Bukharin, Rykov, and Yagoda, who stood accused of an expanded version of the usual set of "Trotskyist crimes," including espionage, sabotage, terrorism, preparation for foreign invasion, the dismemberment of the USSR, the overthrow of Soviet power, and the restoration of capitalism. Previously, Trotskyists had only conspired with the German and Japanese secret services, but now they were accused of cooperating with British and Polish intelligence services as well.

On the basis of Leninist principles, the imperialists were always trying to destroy the only workers-peasants' state in the world, so if they'd planned to destroy it, it was only natural to assume their intelligence services would actively work against the Soviet Union. In Stalin's opinion, it would be "absurd and stupid" to believe external enemies of the USSR would not attack him at their first opportunity, and those who did not share Stalin's conspiracy theories were immediately considered "enemies of the people."

With the government and army thoroughly cleansed of opposition, Stalin attacked the Communist Secret Police. In July 1938, Lavrenty Beria, the head of the

Transcaucasian NKVD, was appointed as the First Deputy under Yezhov, and after that, the real power gradually passed into the hands of Beria. Beria was charged with ferreting out what he called "fascist elements" that he claimed had infiltrated the police force. In reality, it was Beria's job to round up those who knew the details behind the recent killing spree and to see to it that they were silenced. In doing this, he had every leader of the police force executed.

Beria

Under Beria, repression was selective, but the hunt for Trotsky continued in full force during this time. Since being exiled, Trotsky had constantly been on the move, including spending four years in Turkey, followed by periods living in France,

Norway, and finally Mexico, where he remained until his death in 1940. He continued to write at a furious pace throughout this period, composing his own history of the 1917 Revolution and a detailed analysis of what he regarded as the perversion of socialism by Stalin's bureaucracy, which he expounded on in detail in his book The Revolution Betrayed (1936). At the same time, he organized an international movement of communists opposed to what was now called "Stalinism", a project that culminated in the creation of the Fourth International as an alternative to the Third International, the global communist organization now controlled by the Soviet state.

Trotsky reading the Militant in exile

Trotsky was a vocal and tireless critic of Stalin's grotesque "show trials," the humiliating convictions of Bolshevik leaders for alleged counter-revolutionary subversion. In the foreword of The Stalin School of Falsification, Trotsky wrote, "THE MOSCOW TRIALS, which so shocked the world, signify the death agony of Stalinism. A political regime constrained to use such methods is doomed. Depending upon external and internal circumstances, this agony may endure for a longer or shorter period of time. But no power in the world can any longer save Stalin and his system. The Soviet regime will either rid itself of the bureaucratic shell or be sucked into the abyss."

It was through this criticism that Trotsky gained his reputation as an advocate of a humane and democratic socialism. Trotsky's earlier writings about the use of Red Terror make that reputation problematic at best and disingenuous and flatly wrong at worst, but Trotskyist organizations did ultimately become an incubator of dissenting, non-doctrinaire leftist movements.

Even though he was exiled half a world away, Stalin feared his rival's growing international status, and he was never squeamish about the need for extreme methods to silence a potential enemy. Trotsky himself seemed prepared for the possibility. In May 1940, a cadre of Spanish and Mexican communists loyal to Stalin, including the important Mexican painter David Alfaro Siqueiros, assaulted Trotsky's home in an attempted hit. Trotsky survived, but he knew this would not be the last attempt against him.

Chapter 12: Trotsky With Supporters In

1940

Trotsky wouldn't be so lucky the second time around. On August 20, 1940, a Stalinist agent of Spanish origin named Ramón Mercader entered Trotsky's home and plunged an ice pick into his skull. Mercader later testified at his trial, "I laid my raincoat on the table in such a way as to be able to remove the ice axe which was in the pocket. I decided not to miss the wonderful opportunity that presented itself. The moment Trotsky began reading the article, he gave me my chance; I took out the ice axe from the raincoat, gripped it in my hand and, with my eyes closed, dealt him a terrible blow on the head."

Incredibly, the badly injured Trotsky was able to fight off his attacker with the help of his bodyguards, but he died the following day. His last words were allegedly, "I will not survive this attack.

Stalin has finally accomplished the task he attempted unsuccessfully before."

The Formation of the KGB

During the Great Patriotic War (the term the Soviets used to refer to the fighting against Nazi Germany during World War II), scientific, political, and military intelligence exerted a great influence on Soviet politics, and the NKVD played a crucial role. According to Soviet estimates, the NKVD had 53 divisions and 28 brigades, "not counting the many independent units and border troops" (Gordievskiy and Andru, 1992), many of which were used as security units to prevent the escape of troops and to carry out punitive operations against "unreliable peoples." A number of minorities, including Chechens, Ingush, Crimean Tatars, Karachais, Balkars, Kalmyks, and Volga Germans, were victims of NKVD mass killings and forced evictions.

In March 1946, the NKGB and NKVD were transformed from commissariats to ministries, which meant raising their status. Later, they were known as the

Ministry of State Security (MGB) and the Ministry of Internal Affairs (MVD), respectively. Viktor Semenovich Abakumov became the head of the MGB. Stalin had expected that Abakumov would limit Beria's influence in the state security agencies, but he was wrong, and Abakumov quickly became a "trusted person of Beria." (ibid). In fact, he never reported to anyone, not even Stalin, without first consulting Beria.

Abakumov's leadership style was marked by cruelty and corruption, but he was friendly and kind with his protégés. In all likelihood, Abakumov was the one who was sensitive about being in the shadow of the Cheka and thus ordered previously sacred relics removed from the memorial room in the officer's club of the MGB. Most notably, Dzerzhinsky's death mask and portrait were removed, and a tradition was established in which officers of the MGB who had traveled abroad expressed their respect to Abakumov with expensive gifts. Immoral behavior and corruption were mentioned among the official reasons for Abakumov's arrest in 1951 and his subsequent execution in 1954.

After World War II, the Soviet Union recognized the United States as its "main enemy." Great Britain, the main object of NKVD interests before the war, became a secondary concern. During the war, when the Soviet Union found itself allied with the U.S. and the British, Russian intelligence was working in the West with less interference than ever before, but once the war ended and the Cold War dawned, Moscow faced new problems. The first, oddly enough, was the demobilization of American and British intelligence units. The decision by President Truman to liquidate the Office of Strategic Services (the predecessor of the CIA) in September 1945 deprived the NKGB and many of their agents of the possibility of penetration into their main enemy's secret services. After the establishment of the Central Intelligence Agency (CIA) in 1947, Soviet intelligence had to start from scratch. Moreover, their penetration into the CIA was much more difficult than penetration into the OSS had been.

By the time the CIA was created in July 1947, many effective verification methods had become widely used that made the introduction of Soviet agents impossible. Soviet intelligence services would be able to inflict the greatest damage on American intelligence via the interception and decipherment of classified intelligence.

While Moscow retained intelligence forces in the West, the West did not have the same opportunities in Moscow. Almost all attempts to penetrate Russia across the border from the Baltic in the north and Turkey in the south failed as a result of Moscow's counterintelligence operations.

The 1950s saw the death of Stalin, the brief stay in power of Beria, the rejection of Stalin's cult of personality by Nikita Khrushchev; the first political "thaw," and the birth of the KGB. Once its structure and principles of activity were formed, it remained mostly unchanged for almost 40 years.

The situation in America had also dynamically been changed. For example, in January 1956, under President Eisenhower's direction, a Council of Consultants was formed to periodically review intelligence issues abroad, and the intelligence apparatus of England was expanded. From 1955-1957, four new departments were created to work against socialist countries. In 1957-1958, a major reorganization of intelligence and counter-intelligence bodies of France was carried out.

One of the main reasons for the reforms was the need to carry out tasks arising from the countries' membership in NATO. On a semi-legal basis, the German intelligence service "The Organization of Gehlen" was included in the structure of the government bodies of West Germany until 1956. In contrast to the first post-war decade, when West Germany had led tactical reconnaissance in Hungary, the GDR, and Czechoslovakia, it now began conducting reconnaissance operations in the territory of the Soviet Union.

After Stalin's death, there was a weakening of the repressive policy toward those who had cooperated with the German occupiers during the Great Patriotic War. In September 1955, the Decree of the Presidium of the Supreme Soviet of the USSR gave amnesty to this category of citizens. Former Soviet citizens who had found themselves abroad now returned to the country.

Between 1955 and 1958, over 12,000 people came home, and foreign special services hastened to use this "channel" to send agents to the Soviet Union. According to author Alexander Sever, "Since 1956, among the immigrants arriving in the USSR, operational officers exposed 30 to 50 foreign intelligence agents and emissaries of anti-Soviet centers and organizations every year. In particular, in 1957, 26 agents of the imperialist intelligence services and 36 participants of foreign anti-Soviet centers and organizations were found among the arriving immigrants."

Not only did the Russian intelligence services have to fight with the external enemies of the Soviet state, they also had to deal with internal enemies, such as "Banderaers" and "forest brothers" who had cooperated with the German invaders. After the Red Army had liberated the territory of Western Ukraine, Belarus, and the Baltic States, they began to terrorize and plunder the local civilian population.

According to the Resolution of the Central Committee of the Communist Party (CPSU) of March 12, 1954, the main operational activities of state security agencies in the latter 1950s included the struggle against destructive activities of the imperialist intelligence services and foreign anti-Soviet centers, the elimination of the remnants of the "bourgeois-nationalist underground" in the territories of Western Ukraine, Belorussia, and the Baltic republics, and the struggle against anti-Soviet elements, such as churchmen, sectarians, and other hostile elements within the country (Sever, 2008). By the beginning of the 1960s, the Soviets had only managed the second task of eliminating the remnants of the "bourgeois-nationalist underground."

The 1950s were also recognized in the Soviet Union as a "period of reforms and reductions." From 1953-1967, the Soviet Union had five leaders, structural and functional changes took place regularly, and massive staff cuts were made. The Central Committee of the CPSU began the process of transforming state security on July 11, 1951, due to " the unfavorable situation in the Ministry of State Security of the USSR." Two days later, the Minister of the MGB, General Viktor Abakumov, lost his position and was arrested. He was replaced by former secretary of the Central Committee of the CPSU, Semyon Ignatiev. The change of the head of the department subsequently led to a series of resignations in the central apparatus and in territorial bodies.

In January 1952, a system of secret informants was eliminated and a new category of special agents was introduced.

That November, the Bureau of the Presidium of the CPSU Central Committee also established a commission to reorganize the intelligence and counter-intelligence services of the MGB USSR. As a result of its activities, the Bureau of the Presidium of the CPSU Central Committee adopted a decision (BP7 / 12-op of December 30, 1952) for the establishment of the Main Intelligence Directorate in the USSR MGB on January 5, 1953, by the order of MGB No. 006, but the project was never implemented due to the death of Stalin in March 1953.

New reforms began after that. At a joint meeting of the Plenum of the CPSU Central Committee, the Council of Ministers of the USSR and the Presidium of the Supreme Soviet of the USSR, a decision was made to merge the MGB and Ministry of Internal Affairs (Ministry of the Interior of the USSR). This move was initiated by Beria. At the same meeting, it was decided to appoint Beria as the First Deputy Chairman of the Council of Ministers of the USSR, and at the same time, Minister

163

of the Interior of the USSR. He held these posts for a short time before being arrested on June 26, 1953, the result of an initiative undertaken by a "group of comrades from the Politburo." Beria was shot on December 23, 1953.

After Beria's arrest, Sergei Kruglov, the new Minister of Internal Affairs, filed an official note to the "instance" (the so-called Central Committee of the CPSU) on February 4, 1954, with a proposal to establish a "Committee for State Security under the Council Ministers of the USSR."

This document was discussed on February 8, 1954, at the Presidium of the Central Committee of the CPSU, and fully approved.

The Committee for State Security ("Komitet Gosudarstvennoy Bezopasnosti" in Russian), was established in accordance with the Decree of the Presidium of the Supreme Soviet of the USSR of March 13, 1954. This date is considered the official date of the KGB's birth, although the Chekists mark the holiday on December 20, the day of the Cheka's creation.

Ivan Serov was appointed the first chairman of the KGB. He had risen rapidly in his career under Stalin and Khrushchev, actively participated in the procedure of rehabilitation of victims of judicial arbitrariness, and by June 1957, had fired more than 18,000 security officers, including 40 generals.

Serov

This wave of personnel changes was completed in February 1956, when Serov "reported" the dismissal of 16,000 employees to the Central Committee of the CPSU "as politically not confiable, violators of socialist legality, careerists, morally unstable, as well as illiterate and backward workers."

The second stage of "cleansing" ended in June 1957, when another 2,000 employees of the central apparatus were dismissed from state security agencies "for violating Soviet legality, abuse of office and immoral acts." There were 48 people who held the posts of heads of departments and other higher positions. As a result, as noted in the certificate prepared by Serov for the (1957) Plenum of the Central Committee, "almost all senior officials of the central administrations, departments of the central apparatus were changed." (Lubyanka, 2003). As a result of personnel cuts, the number of State Security Committee workers decreased in 1957 by half compared to 1954. Moving forward, Serov would rely both on old Chekists and new party nominees.

Under Serov, the tasks and responsibilities of the KGB's central apparatus and its local bodies were clearly formulated:

a)   intelligence work in capitalist countries;

b)   combating espionage, sabotage, terrorist, and other subversive activities of foreign intelligence agencies, foreign anti-

Soviet centers, and their agents inside the country;

c)   the struggle against anti-Soviet activities and nationalist elements within the USSR;

d)   counter-intelligence work in the Soviet Army, the Navy, GVF (Civil Air Fleet), border troops, and the troops of the Ministry of Interior in order to prevent the penetration of foreign intelligence agents and other enemy elements into their ranks;

e)   counter-intelligence work at special facilities and in the sphere of transport;

f)   state border protection of the USSR;

g)   protection of party and government leaders;

h)   organization and provision of government communications;

i)   the organization of radio-reconnaissance work; [and]

j)   [the] development of mobilization plans for the deployment of the state security organs and the military units of the Committee and the fulfilment of other assignments of the Central Committee of the CPSU and the Government of the USSR.

In this document, the rights of state security bodies were defined:

a)   to have necessary agents to conduct operational works in order to identify and suppress hostile activities directed against the Soviet Union;

b)   produce and legally establish searches, detentions and arrests of persons convicted or suspected of criminal activities;

c)   to conduct an investigation in cases of state crimes, committed by officers, sergeants, servants and workers of the KGB;

d)   to carry out special measures aimed at detecting the criminal activity of foreign intelligence agents and anti-Soviet elements;

e)   in cases of necessity, in coordination with police chiefs, to involve the police in order to ensure the fulfilment of the tasks of state security bodies;

f) to keep operative records of state criminals and persons who are suspected of belonging to foreign intelligence agencies, participation in anti-Soviet organizations, and other hostile activities;

g) to check the state of the encryption service and secret records management in ministries and departments, as well as subordinate enterprises and institutions;

h) to carry out a special inspection of persons with careers in relation to state and military secrets, as well as those who go abroad and back to the USSR; [and]

i) publish literature, training, and visual aids on matters within the competence of the Committee (Shevyakin, 2004).

Over the course of its history, the activities of the KGB were regulated by more than 5,000 different normative acts approved by the Council of Ministers of the USSR. According to contemporaries of Serov, he was an agile, proactive, hard-working person who used to demand rapid decision-making from his subordinates. He listened to the opinion of famous scientists, retained departmental patriotism, and did not allow for further reduction of the central apparatus. The main reason for his resignation from his post as chairman of the KGB on December 8, 1958, was based on his complicated relationship with the USSR's highest party leadership.

The allocation of state security agencies to a separate department required the establishment of a special KGB award. Thus, on December 6, 1957, on the 40th anniversary of the bodies, a badge of the Honorary State Security Officer was established to be awarded "for the concrete results achieved in operational performance" in accordance with the decision of the board of the Committee.

After the reorganization of the Ministry of Internal Affairs and the formation of the KGB under the Council of Ministers of the USSR, counter-intelligence was renamed the Second Main Directorate of the KGB (VGU). At that point, security officers had to completely reorganize their work. If earlier foreign secret services actively used their agents in the territory of the Soviet Union through illegal channels, now they preferred legal means of "delivering" them to the territory of the Soviet Union. Naturally, the Soviets assumed the best place to find foreign spies would be among embassy employees, tourists, journalists, and businessmen. In 1955 and the first half of 1956, the Soviets exposed more than 40 foreign spies "among American, British, French and other delegation participants."

The sphere of interests had also been changed. Now, the object of their increased attention was the sphere of nuclear energy, the creation of hydrogen weapons, and rocketry. The wide use of the latest radio electronic equipment, pulsed radio navigation, and radar devices was used. By 1956, foreign intelligence had switched to one-way radio communication with its agents. Microphotography was also widely used. A popular way of contacting agents working under diplomatic cover in the territory of the Soviet Union was the use of systems of impersonal communication. All of this greatly complicated the identification of enemy agents.

In 1954, a strengthening of the intelligence apparatus was carried out, excluding agents who did not inspire confidence and who were incapable of assisting the KGB authorities with their personal qualities and counter-intelligence capabilities. In 1955, the KGB issued Order No. 00420, "On Improving Agency Work," which aimed "to recruit persons with higher and secondary education who possessed the necessary personal qualities and operational capabilities to conduct spy and other subversive activities, to search for state criminals and solve other counter-intelligence tasks" (Abramov, 2006).

In July 1954, the USSR Ministry of Foreign Affairs announced that Military Assistant and Attache of the U.S. Embassy in Moscow Howard Felchlin and Military Assistant and Attache of the US Embassy Major Walter McKinney were "persona non grata." These men traveled through the territory of the Soviet Union on a regular basis and were actively engaged in spying. During one trip, Felchlin and McKinney forgot espionage records denouncing their true activities in their train compartment. The next month, the USSR Ministry of Foreign Affairs sent protest notes to the U.S. Embassy in Moscow about the systematic attempts of the two men to penetrate the area of military facilities. In May 1955, the U.S. military assistants in Moscow, Colonel John Benson, Captain William Strode, and Captain Walter Mühle, were named "persona non grata" in connection with the fact they had made extensive trips to Soviet territory and were actively collecting spy information.

In January 1957, U.S. military assistants in Moscow Major Hubert Tensei and Captain Charles Stockel were also expelled from the Soviet Union after they allegedly made repeated attempts to penetrate areas where military units, airfields and other military facilities were located. In 1958, the Second Secretary of the U.S. Embassy was forced to leave, and in 1959, the First Secretary of the U.S. Embassy, David Mark, also left,

At the end of the 1950s, the CIA began to actively involve American scientists in the gathering of information about the Soviet Union's achievements and plans in the field of rocket science. They received intelligence data during meetings with Soviet colleagues in what the Americans called "Operation Lincoln." The operation, which came to involve over 100 people, was considered a partial success.

By 1963, the CIA would seek to collect information on every major development in Soviet science and technology, and the reaction of the KGB was immediate. Already in the early 1950s, American and British intelligence had undertaken a series of unsuccessful attempts to collect information on the Soviet nuclear industry. Most often, the collection of information was entrusted to agent-parachutists, but almost all of them were quickly identified and arrested without the time to get the information back. After

Stalin's death and the partial weakening of the counter-intelligence regime, foreign diplomats increasingly began to participate in operations seeking to uncover Soviet atomic secrets. In this, NATO partners did not lag behind the United States. For example, British intelligence began to conduct "Operation Legal Traveler," with the main objective of collecting water and air samples to determine areas for testing nuclear weapons, as well as identifying objects associated with its production and storage, which involved English tourists, businessmen, and scientists who had legally entered the territory of the Soviet Union.

Strengthening the KGB

There was no major change in the KGB until 1967, apart from minor structural changes in the fall of 1966, when the Accounting and Archival Division became the Tenth Division. The group under the KGB Chairman for the study and generalization of the work experience of state security bodies was transformed into a group of assistants, and the Eleventh Division, responsible for coordinating communications with state security organs of the socialist countries, was created. As an independent unit, it did not last long.

Despite frequent changes of KGB chairmen, the state security agencies survived the crisis provoked by the personnel and structural reforms of the mid-1950s. With that, the KGB became more active in the roles of protecting state and military secrets. On October 1, 1965, a new "instruction to ensure the safety of state secrets and the regime of secrecy of ongoing work" was approved.

On May 18, 1967, Yuri Andropov was named the new Secretary of the CPSU Central Committee. He remained in this post for 15 years, longer than any other colleague in Soviet times, and he immensely boosted the KGB's reputation, despite the fact he would be blamed by the public for the Soviets' costly fighting in Afghanistan in the 1980s. The Fifth Department of the KGB was created by Andropov to organize counter-intelligence work and combat the ideological sabotage in the country. In fact, any important appointment could only take place with the approval of the State Security Committee in all spheres, from the ministry to industry, from art to sports.

At the same time, there was an improvement in operational search activities. For example, in 1964, the "instruction on the procedure for carrying out operational and technical measures in the practice of the operative-intelligence and investigation work of the KGB" was adopted. In particular, this allowed the use of "Providence," complex operational measures, to confirm the connection of GRU officer Oleg Penkovsky with British and US intelligence services.

"Operation 100," a plan of agent and operational activities, had been developed to increase the level of counter-intelligence work among foreigners in 1965. Initially, it covered the European part of the country and the Caucasus, but eventually it spread to Central Asia. The purpose of this plan was to coordinate the actions of counter-intelligence units on a national scale.

Based on the experience of "Operation 100," a prospective counterintelligence work plan was developed in 1967 called "Operation Horizon." That year, amongst foreigners who had come to the USSR for a short time, more than 250 officers and agents of special services of foreign states were identified. Over 100 of them were convicted and expelled from the USSR.

There was much progress in the fight against corruption. Andropov's subordinates earned huge wages for the time, but they were strongly punished in cases of corruption. Also under his leadership, special detachments "Alpha" and "Vympel" were created to destroy terrorists and release hostages.

In accordance with the tasks set by the June (1967) Plenum of the Central Committee of the CPSU, the main focus of the KGB was above all else to strengthen foreign policy, to contribute to the successful implementation of Soviet foreign policy to ensure timely identification, and the exposure of the subversive plans of imperialist states and their intelligence agencies. One of the first steps in this direction was the strengthening of the intelligence service by experienced Chekists, both in the central apparatus and abroad.

Following the instructions of the CPSU Central Committee, the KGB carried out a series of measures to strengthen the fight against the anti-Soviet activities of Chinese opponents of Communism and ensure the reliable protection of the Soviet border with China. The KGB worked to establish several intelligence units in the territories and regions bordering China.

Giving high priority to the timely receipt of secret information about the subversive intentions of the enemies, the KGB intelligence service took steps to enhance their agents' positions, primarily in the U.S. Strengthening the intelligence apparatus of the intelligence service helped to obtain important information on political, military, scientific, and technical problems. The main attention in the matter of increasing the level of counter-intelligence work in the country was focused on further improvements to countering military, economic, and political espionage.

Thanks to this work, the KGB would successfully identify many operations carried out by enemy intelligence services in certain areas of the Soviet Union, particularly the Far East, the Baltic countries, and the border regions of the Ukraine. The counter-intelligence service carried out operations resulting in the photographing of 54 documents of ambassadors to NATO member countries, annual reports of some military attaches to other embassies, classified materials on political, military-economic, operational, and other issues.

Measures to identify and suppress the hostile activities of anti-Soviet elements among churchmen and sectarians were also undertaken, taking into account the ideologically harmful activities of religious and Zionist centers. 122 KGB agents were sent abroad to reveal their intentions, to disrupt the subversive actions they had prepared, and to carry out other counter-intelligence assignments.

At the same time, it was possible to attribute criminal liability for illegal activities to a number of active sectarians. According to official KGB reports in 1975, the main efforts were focused on "improving measures to effectively counter the enemy's intelligence aspirations, reliable protection of state and military secrets, and suppression of hostile ideological sabotage."

On July 5, 1978, the KGB under the USSR Council of Ministers was renamed the USSR State Security Committee, but the system and structure of the KGB bodies remained unchanged. The second half of the 1970s and the beginning of the 1980s did not differ significantly from the previous period, and Andropov was still the chairman of the KGB.

In 1978, foreign intelligence received documents and other valuable materials regarding the foreign and domestic policies of the United States and China, as well as their subversive activities against the USSR and the Warsaw Bloc countries. The activities of the governing bodies of NATO were also covered.

As this all makes clear, at the height of the Cold War, the KGB focused its attention not on the repression of USSR dissidents, but on countering the activities of foreign special services. That said, Andropov also actively opposed the emergence of nationalist and church-sectarian organizations. The head of the KGB named certain representatives of the Catholic, Jewish, and Muslim clergy, as well as leaders of such sects as Baptists, Seventh Day Adventists, Jehovah's Witnesses, and Pentecostals, as the main ideological opponents. In this regard, the attention of the fifth KGB units was directed to the timely suppression of the activities of the emissaries of the foreign missions of these sects. There were many other religious organizations whose activities were prohibited in the Soviet Union, such as

"Underground Evangelism" (USA), "Light in the East" (FRG), "Institute for the Study of Religion and Communism" (England), "Friedenstimme" (FRG), "Foreign Mission of the Council of Churches of the European Baptist Church" (USA), etc.

Special attention was paid by Andropov to Zionism, considering the Soviet Union had mostly allied with the Arab world as the West supported Israel. In his opinion, the enemies of the USSR actively used Zionism and specific pro-Zionist elements for subversive purposes.

Elimination

By the beginning of the 1980s, the Soviet Union seriously lagged behind the advanced Western countries. The civilian branches of the economy developed extremely slowly, with billions of rubles spent on the arms race and the maintenance of the army. The outdated political system also hampered the development of the country.

In 1985, the Soviet Union was headed by Mikhail Gorbachev, an energetic leader who announced the beginning of perestroika, intended to accelerate economic growth by absorbing new technologies and by strengthening discipline and people's interest in the results of their work. In foreign policy, Gorbachev expressed his support for a new course, which he labeled "new thinking." The USSR became less confrontational with the West, and negotiations were held with President Reagan. During these meetings, agreements were reached on the relaxation of international tension and the reduction of nuclear stockpiles.

CPSIA information can be obtained
at www.ICGtesting.com
Printed in the USA
BVHW050141140223
658390BV00012B/438